D0982617

THE
RUNNING TRIVIA
BOOK

THE
RUNNING
TRIVIA
BOOK

1001 Questions from the Sprints to the Marathon

Mark Will-Weber

BREAKAWAY BOOKS
HALCOTTSVILLE, NEW YORK
2005

The Running Trivia Book: 1001 Questions from the Sprints to the Marathon
Copyright 2005 by Mark Will-Weber

ISBN: 1-891369-57-1

Published by Breakaway Books
P.O. Box 24
Halcottsville, NY 12438
(800) 548-4348
www.breakawaybooks.com

FIRST EDITION

CONTENTS

INTRODUCTION

In the Comrades Marathon, which is actually an ultramarathon of more than 50 miles, there's a section of the course descriptively known as "the Valley of 1,000 Hills."

In the late going of this project, sometimes I felt as if I was laboring there—trudging along, up one hill down another, knowing that I had already run far, but well aware that I still had a multitude of miles to go before I could claim victory. This arduous task brought to mind what William Shakespeare wrote in *Richard II:* "These high wild hills and rough uneven ways draw out our miles and make them wearisome."

In truth, during rare, dire moments I began to refer to this book project as "The Beast" and dreamed of driving a stake through its heart . . . to put it to rest, wrapped in a blanket of finality.

Nevertheless, most of the challenge proved enlightening: I was learning facts about my sport. Sometimes it was trivial stuff that I had forgotten about. But often the search unearthed new facts and aspects about running that had somehow eluded me, despite more than three decades in this sport as a writer, runner, and coach. I spent time looking around at this vast material—1,000 hills or 1,000 questions, both loom with a certain formidableness—and admired the beauty of our sport. Some of the questions/answers brought a smile to my face—and a select few actually had tears welling up in my eyes, or brought on a dull ache down in my throat. Sometimes, even long after I had snapped up the particular question and answer I was hunting down, I willingly meandered down an interesting side path because the subject I had stumbled upon proved so compelling.

In fact, even when I finally surrendered the manuscript—having staggered across the agreed-upon finish line of 1000-plus questions—I still discovered a dozen or so glittering nuggets that all but demanded to be included in the trivia treasure chest. In essence, a book like this could be almost never-ending, since it is virtually a reflection of the history of running—the athletes, the coaches, the famous races—that make what appears to be such a simplistic activity brim with both interest and inspiration.

What was I looking for exactly? Consider each question as a piece of colored thread—some more eye-catching than others—that, when woven together, might create a tapestry that helped tell the story of running, from sprints to the marathon.

What is the perfect trivia question? Arguably a question that *nearly* turns on "the light" in the reader's mind; a question that produces that look—a thoughtful squint, a chin held by a hand—that says: "I think I know this! Don't tell me!"

Questions, of course, can be too obscure. For example, it wouldn't be fair of me to ask: "What world-class milers once stopped for a pizza at my house in Bethlehem, Pennsylvania, back in the 1980s?" Answer: John Walker of New Zealand, first man to break 3:50 in the mile, and Steve Scott, still (as of this writing) the U.S.-record holder in the mile. Pete Heesen (himself an NCAA Division II champ in cross-country and the steeplechase), my former college teammate and once one of Steve Scott's training partners, simply showed up on my doorstep with them one day. I tried to pay for the pizza and Walker wouldn't even allow me to do that: "Don't be bloody silly, mate . . . I've got it."

Obviously, there are some people who could more than hold their own answering the vast majority of questions in this book. Some might even make light work of it——a guy like Dave Johnson (former *Track & Field News* staffer and now director of the Penn Relays); my former *Runner's World* colleague Marty Post; Roger Robinson of New Zealand (runner, author of *Running in Literature,* college literature professor); and a select few other quiz wizards would seem to have "the right stuff." Surely they would score well on *Running Trivia* if put to the test. But it also begs the question: Would someone like Roger Robinson be able to come up with the track trivia reference in the rap song "Baby Got Back" by Sir Mix-A-Lot? Perhaps, but certainly his chances improve dramatically on questions concerning William Blake and poetry and a certain connection to the title of a famous running film.

We all have our strengths and weaknesses, but what I hope most is that this book—like *The Quotable Runner* published by Breakaway Books 10 years earlier—simply enhances the enjoyment and universality of our sport of running. And, too, I wanted it to celebrate the courage of our sport—like Terry Fox dipping his leg in the Atlantic Ocean and heading west on his "Marathon of Hope." It helps to remember, especially when the days seem most dark, that we are (to quote Sir Winston Churchill) not made of sugar candy.

—Mark Will-Weber, September 2005

STARTING LINES

(The roots and traditions of running)

In his work *Dissertations,* the Stoic philosopher Epictetus (1st-2nd century AD) observed just how much a man had to put up with simply to enjoy the pinnacle of sport—the Olympic Games.

"There are enough troublesome and irksome things in life; aren't things just as bad at the Olympic festival?" he wrote. "Aren't you scorched there by the fierce heat? Aren't you crushed in the crowd. . . . Aren't you bothered by the noise, the din and other nuisances? But it seems to me that you are well able to bear and indeed gladly endure all this, when you think of the gripping spectacles that you will see."

One can only hope that ticket prices were more reasonable in Epictetus's era.

As for the athletes themselves, it's been a slow evolution from the pioneer days of running to what we see today. For example, even as late as the 1970s all-weather tracks remained a rarity; today, it's not unusual to see them at the high school level.

Bob Schul, one of America's Olympic heroes at the Tokyo Games in '64, maintains that he might have clocked very close to 13 minutes for 5,000 meters when he was at his best, had he had access to all-weather surfaced tracks. The difference, theorizes Schul (who once ran 13:38 with a 54-second last lap), might have been worth 2 seconds per lap.

Shoes weren't exactly high-tech. Ask some of the "old-timers" about the clunky footwear they were often forced to endure—and that was if they could even afford to buy shoes to race in.

Emil Zatopek, the great Czech runner, did a lot of his training in army boots, knowing he could always get another pair when the leather wore out. Besides, his racing shoes felt so much lighter when he laced them up for competition.

Success didn't necessarily boot you up to a higher class of shoe, either. Consider Englishman Jim Peters's lament:

"At the start of the 1947 season I was just besieged with invitations to run. . . . But hardly had the season opened when I got badly blistered feet through wearing poorly made spikes. At this time, I was still not in a position to buy a really expensive hand-made pair—even though I was the national six-mile champion."

Still, there was an undeniable purity to the sport in its earliest days. Full-time athletes were rare (professionals, like the England's Walter George, who ran just under 4:13 for the mile in 1886), and runners tended to be either young students or working-class heroes blowing off steam away from the job. A classic example would have been multi-time Boston Marathon winner Clarence DeMar, who worked as a typesetter when he wasn't trying to win long-distance races.

Amby Burfoot, my former boss at *Runner's World* magazine, tells me that both cross-country races and the steeplechase event can trace their roots back to England. Apparently some Englishmen used to enjoy racing—hell-bent-for-leather—on their horses from village to village (spying a village church steeple in the distance as a guide), jumping fences at more than just a little peril to life and limb, and—one assumes after more than a few broken collarbones and legs—deciding that perhaps this "cross-country" racing stuff might be better conducted by runners, sans equine.

Needless to say, man's running, in the survival context of the word, probably goes back to the beginning of human (and proto-human) time. The ancient Inca peoples of South America used messengers (called *chasqui*) to deliver coded messages (called *quipus*) to the Inca king. According to some research, these messengers—using a relay system—could cover as much as 200 miles in a day, despite rugged terrain and the high altitudes of the Andes Mountains.

Sport, of course, is often an offshoot of necessity. Running is no exception. And—when considering the field events—it doesn't take a lot of imagination to figure out what purpose the javelin or the hammer served in its pre-sport life.

1. The English "pioneers" of the organized sport we now call cross-country didn't mess around. This 10-mile cross-country event—called the Crick Run—dates back to 1838 and (despite its name that would suggest a different sport) began at this site in Warwickshire.

A. Archery Academy; B. Rugby School; C. Cricket Academy; D. the Riding School

2. True or False. College track and cross-country meets in America were already being contested before 1880.

3. True or False. Organized cross-country races on England's Wimbledon Green predate lawn tennis.

4. **SILVER-MEDAL QUESTION.** This British runner, who set many records at various middle and long distances between 1900 and 1920, was one of the very first to record his training methods and advice in book form.

5. **BRONZE-MEDAL QUESTION.** One of the first organized school cross-country races in America occurred at this Massachusetts prep school in 1891.

A: Germantown Academy; B. Blair Academy; C. Mount Hermon; D. Princeton Day School

6. What delicious prizes are given out to runners as awards in this ongoing cross-country event?

A. roasted potatoes; B. baked pies; C. corn fritters; D. homemade doughnuts

7. What famous runner graduated from the school that hosts this more-than-a-century-old event?

A. Amby Burfoot; B. Bill Rodgers; C. Frank Shorter; D. Bob Kennedy

8. True or False. Running games such as "Hounds and Hares" and "Paper Trail" were two forerunners of cross-country in some places.

9. True or False. In the 1880s Madison Square Garden hosted numerous multiday "go-as-you-please" (run, walk) races, including even some six-day events.

10. The first NCAA Division I track meet for men took place in 1921 at this midwestern university's Stagg Stadium. The University of Illinois won the inaugural meet.

A. Notre Dame; B. Michigan; C. University of Chicago; D. North Dakota

11. True or False. The Penn Relays is more than 110 years old.

12. Medals and awards at the Penn Relays often depict this figure of the American Revolution bestowing honors upon half-naked relay runners.

A. Samuel Adams; B. Ben Franklin; C. George Washington; D. Paul Revere

13. True or False. A Kansas student who transferred to the University of Pennsylvania, and saw the Penn Relays there, brought the idea of that meet back to his home state—and thus launched the Kansas Relays in 1923.

14. *Runner's World* magazine was in full upswing by 1970. The original name of the publication, however, was:

A. Run, Jog, Walk; B. *Fun & Fitness Running;* C. *Celebrity Running;* D. *Distance Running News*

15. The publication was founded on a shoestring budget by:

A. Bob Anderson; B. Bert Nelson; C. Hal Higdon; D. Joe Henderson

16. This U.S. publication is sub-titled *The Bible of the Sport.*

17. NCAA Division I track men first motored around an indoor track in this city in 1965. Missouri won the first indoor title.

A. Indianapolis, Indiana; B. Boston, Massachusetts; C. New York City; D. Detroit

18. The first modern Olympic Games were staged in this city:

A. Athens, Greece; B. Berlin, Germany; C. Paris, France; D. London, England

19. What was the year of the first modern Olympic Games?

A. 1875; B. 1896; C. 1900; D. 1904

20. True or False. The first official gold medal winner of the Olympic Games was a former Harvard student who quit school to compete.

21. True or False. Some runners in the first modern Olympic Games refused to compete in their final events because they were scheduled for Sunday.

22. True or False. Footmen in England—who often ran ahead of their employers riding in the coach—became some of the first professional runners, with much wagering on the outcomes.

23. Professional races drew lots of betting action in England and often took place on tracks near:

A. the village square; B. Wimbledon; C. cricket pitches; D. public houses or "pubs" (bars)

24. Some of the very first documented professional races in America (dating back to the early 1800s) were staged in this New Jersey city, just across the river from New York City.

A. Atlantic City; B. Hoboken; C. Cherry Hill; D. Newark

25. In the 1860s one of the most famous professional runners was an Indian man named Lewis Bennett. He was a particular favorite on the English racing circuit, but he was better known by his nickname:

A. the Running Wolf; B. the Bronze Warrior; C. the Sprinting Seneca; D. Deerfoot

26. In 1928 a barnstorming coast-to-coast professional footrace that began in California and finished in New York got the starting gun. A game and gutsy Oklahoman named (fittingly) Andy Payne dispatched the 3,400-plus miles in a mere 84 days and won a princely sum (in those days) of $25,000. What was this novel event called?

A. the Cross-America Ramble; B. the Bunion Derby; C. the Blister Blitz; D. the Transcontinental Trot

27. Of the nearly 200 runners who started this literal "cross-country" run, how many finished?

A. All of them; B. 101; C. 45; D. less than a dozen

28. True or False. One of the origins of both the term *steeplechase* and the actual event may have come from cross-country races in England where competitors jumped gates and used church steeples in distant villages to mark the course.

29. True or False. The marathon was one of the most important events of the ancient Olympic Games in Greece and usually finished at an important structure, such as the Acropolis.

30. True or False. Ancient Olympians were pure amateurs. The only awards they accepted were olive wreaths placed upon their brows in victory.

31. True or False. Women were barred from competing in the ancient Olympic Games.

32. True or False. Baron Pierre de Coubertin was one of the first supporters of allowing women to compete in the Olympic Games.

33. In what Olympic Games did women finally compete?

A. 1908; B. 1924; C. 1936; D. 1948

34. True or False. Greek sprinters in the ancient Games often raced in their armor and with their battle shields.

35. True or False. A converted Christian put an end to the Olympic Games because he believed them to be "pagan" in nature.

36. The site of the ancient Games in Olympia was unearthed by:

A. Avery Brundage, the future Olympic president; B. Baron Pierre de Coubertin and a team of French archaeologists; C. a team of German archaeologists in 1875; D. American archaeologist Dr. Indiana Jones in 1910

37. Although there were no stands at Olympia, evidence suggests that the ancient Games drew this many spectators—most of whom simply sat on the grassy hillsides.

A. 10,000; B. 20,000; C. 45,000; D. 100,000

38. True or False. Baron Pierre de Coubertin's heart is buried in a sacred grove in Olympia, Greece, and the rest of his body is buried

in Lausanne, Switzerland.

39. The bulk of the American contingent made its way to Athens aboard the ship *Gibraltar.* What happened to several of the team members en route?

A. They were attacked by sharks while swimming in the Port of Piraeus; B. They suffered food poisoning and were unable to compete in the Games; C. They suffered severe cases of sunburn and were less than 100 percent when they competed; D. They were injured when a very large wave crashed over the ship

40. At the 1896 Olympic Games in Athens, competitors from other nations were intrigued by American 400-meter runner Thomas Burke from Boston University because:

A. He raced in shorts instead of pants that covered the knees; B. He brought homemade starting blocks to the line; C. He displayed the rarely-before-seen "crouch start"; D. He wore sunglasses

41. True or False. In some of the earliest track meets, lanes were sometimes separated by ropes or string.

42. In 1908 the Olympic Games were supposed to be held in Rome, Italy. But they were switched to London, England, instead because:

A. Italy had suffered numerous natural disasters, including volcanic eruptions, severe earthquakes, and floods; B. the Italian Olympic Committee was bankrupt; C. There was civil war in Italy between rising Fascist and Socialist factions; D. the railroad workers and dockworkers were on a yearlong strike

43. Latin Lesson. The Olympic motto: *Citius—Altius—Fortius* translates to what?

44. What Olympic bureaucratic big shot (a millionaire himself) exclaimed: "The devotion of the true amateur athlete is the same devotion that makes an artist starve in his garret rather than commercialize his work"?

A. Sir Arthur Gold of Great Britain; B. Avery Brundage of the U.S.A; C. Baron Pierre de Coubertin of France; D. Lord Killanin of Ireland

45. When Jim Thorpe won the decathlon (and a pentathlon, too) at the 1912 Olympic Games in Stockholm, King Gustav V of Sweden declared to him: "You, sir, are the greatest athlete in the world!" To which Jim Thorpe replied:

A. "Thanks, King"; B. "It took ten buckets of sweat, Your Highness"; C. "I had good coaches, sir"; D. "I'm going to Disney World!"

46. Jim Thorpe lost his gold medals, a bronze bust in the likeness of King Gustav V, and a bejeweled replica of a Viking ship after it was discovered that:

A. he had false-started in the 100-meter dash; B. he had played semipro baseball for a few dollars; C. he had sold his autograph for money in the Olympic Village; D. he allowed his name to be used as an endorsement for chewing tobacco

47. Years later, what U.S. president wrote to the Olympic committee and beseeched them (at the time, without success) to restore Jim Thorpe's awards to his family?

A. Richard Nixon; B. Lyndon Baines Johnson; C. Jimmy Carter; D. Gerald Ford

48. Jim Thorpe was eventually buried in a small, picturesque Pennsylvania town on the Lehigh River, now called—as part of the agreement for the famous athlete to be interred there—"Jim Thorpe." What was the town's name *before* it became Jim Thorpe?

A. Warrior's Run; B. Beaver Falls; C. Mauch Chunk; D. Decathlon

49. **GOLD-MEDAL QUESTION.** In the 1912 Olympic Games, what future military hero competed in the military pentathlon

event (just missing a medal) and needed to be revived after he collapsed from all-out exertion in the cross-country run before King Gustav V's royal box?

A. John Pershing; B. Omar Bradley; C. George Smith Patton; D. Dwight Eisenhower

50. The 1916 Olympic Games—canceled because of World War I—were scheduled to be held in what city?

A. Rome; B. Berlin; C. London; D. Dublin

51. True or False. During World I, Baron Pierre de Coubertin lost much of his wealth and moved to Switzerland where the cost of living was cheaper.

52. The Olympic rings first became a symbol for the Games in what year?

A. 1892; B. 1920; C. 1936; D. 1948

53. The five interlocking rings—a symbol of world unification—are meant to represent what geographic landmasses?

54. The Olympic torch relay and torch lightning—two very popu-

lar Olympic traditions—first occurred in what Olympic Games?

A. 1896; B. 1936; C. 1968; D. 1976

55. Exactly how is the Olympic flame in Greece ignited?

56. The release of the Olympic doves is meant to symbolize what still-unrealized dream?

57. At the 1988 Seoul Olympic Games, what mishap messed up one of the Olympic traditions?

A. The Olympic torch went out and had to be relit; B. the Olympic flags were mistakenly raised upside down; C. the Olympic cauldron was lit after the doves were released—resulting in some inadvertently cooked doves; D. the band forgot the notes to the Olympic anthem

58. The 1940 Olympic Games—canceled because of World War II—were scheduled to be held in this city.

A. Warsaw, Poland; B. Berlin, Germany; C. New York City, U.S.A.; D. Tokyo, Japan

59. One of the most historic moments in track history occurred

when this man set three world records and tied a fourth in about an hour at a college track meet.

A. Jim Thorpe; B. James Lightbody; C. Carl Lewis; D. Jesse Owens

60. This event occurred in what meet?

A. The Penn Relays; B. The NCAA Championships; C. The Big Ten Championships; D. The Drake Relays

61. Two of the U.S.A.'s most successful early Olympic track athletes were Alvin Kraenzlein (who made some of the first improvements in hurdling technique) and John Walter Tewksbury, both multi-medal winners. They both represented what Pennsylvania college?

A. The University of Pennsylvania; B. Bloomsburg State; C. Kutztown State; D. Penn State

62. Traditionally, this country is the first to march into the Olympic stadium.

63. True or False. The U.S. contingent has never "dipped" its flag before a foreign leader at the Olympic Games.

64. True or False. At the first modern Olympic Games, the track was less than 400 meters around, had very sharp turns, and the runners ran in a clockwise direction.

65. Participants in the 1948 London Olympic Games were asked to:

A. shake hands before every event; B. bring their own food; C. receive ribbons instead of medals; D. bow their heads in prayer prior to each award ceremony

66. This promising young Australian runner carried the Olympic torch in 1956 for the Melbourne Games.

67. At the 1952 Olympic Games in Helsinki, the crowd roared when this man ran in with the Olympic torch. It seems slightly out of character for this former great known for his somewhat icy demeanor.

68. In his sport they call running "road work." But he once claimed he was "so fast that I can turn out the light and be in bed before the room gets dark." He lit the Olympic cauldron at the 1996 Atlanta Olympic Games to a roaring ovation.

69. True or False. A typical Olympic gold medal these days is actually more than 90 percent silver.

70. This Greek goddess of victory is often depicted on Olympic medals.

A. Aphrodite; B. Hera; C. Nike; D. Helen of Troy

STARTING LINES
ANSWERS

1. B
2. True. In 1876 the Intercollegiate Association of Amateur Athletics contested its championship in men's track, with Princeton taking top honors.
3. True. By 1866 there were cross-country races at Wimbledon. The racket and net stuff came along several years later.
4. Alf Shrubb
5. C
6. B
7. C
8. True. In 1886 some New England students reported "we had a paper chase that went 18 miles . . . some of the other fellows were a little stiff."
9. True
10. C. Chicago. It was held there every year until 1934.
11. True. The Penn Relays was first run in 1895, one year before the first modern Olympic Games.
12. B
13. True. Dr. John Outland, "the Father of the Relays," was the man with the plan.
14. D

15. A

16. *Track & Field News*

17. D

18. A

19. B

20. True. Refused a leave of absence by the college, James B. Connelly paid his own way to Athens and won the first final—the hop, skip, jump.

21. True

22. True

23. D

24. B

25. D

26. B

27. C

28. True

29. False. For some of the earliest competitions, it appears that the longest race was typically one "stade"—about 200 meters. There is some evidence that in later years there were races as long as 2.5 miles.

30. False. Three-time winners sometimes had statues erected in their honor. There were gifts and sometimes even tax exemptions.

31. True. They could be put to death if they were even seen at the Games.

32. False. As late as 1935, the baron stated that women's "primary role should be . . . the crowning of victors with laurels."

33. B. Women finally got the "green light" in a few events at the 1924 Olympic Games in Amsterdam.

34. True

35. True. Roman Emperor Theodosius I ordered the Games abolished, claiming they had become a nuisance to the people.
36. C
37. C
38. True
39. D
40. C
41. True
42. A
43. "Faster—Higher—Stronger"
44. B
45. A
46. B
47. D
48. C
49. C
50. B
51. True
52. B
53. The five continents—The Americas (North and South counting as one), Africa, Asia, Europe, and Australia
54. B
55. An actress, portraying the role of the ancient priestess, uses a mirror to reflect rays from the sun to ignite the flame.
56. World peace
57. C
58. D
59. D
60. C
61. A

62. Greece

63. False. There is strong evidence that the flag was dipped in the 1912 and 1924 Games.

64. True

65. B. The budget was tight and food somewhat scarce in the years after World War II.

66. Ron Clarke

67. Paavo Nurmi

68. Muhammad Ali

69. True. But each "gold" medal—made primarily of silver—must be coated with at least six grams of 24-K gold.

70. C

CROSS-COUNTRY

Cross-country always was my favorite sport, at least when it was going reasonably well. It's just so pure, so natural. As Juha Vaatainen, one of Finland's top runners, once said: "Stadiums are for spectators. We runners have nature and that is much better."

Of course, the truly famous cross-country courses—Van Cortlandt Park and Franklin Park certainly being a pair that immediately comes to mind—take on the same venerable status of a Yankee Stadium, a Fenway Park, a Wrigley Field. If the trees are bursting with the yellow, red, and burnt orange leaves of fall—the season when cross-country flourishes—then our "stadiums" brim with unconfined beauty. I personally prefer a cross-country route that's *not* run around the manicured fairways of a closely clipped golf course, but, yes, they, too, can be pleasing to a spectator's eye. (The actual cross-country runners, of course, dealing with the demands of racing, may be less enamored with the visuals until the finish line has been crossed.)

Nature, of course, can throw you some knuckleballs, so to speak. Like the time in 1997 when the NCAA Division III Championships were staged at Franklin Park in Boston. Snow and rain and mud made for an interesting, shoe-sucking course. We wrapped rolls and rolls of white trainer's tape around the shoes of our runners to make sure they stayed on their feet. A gray sky spit some sort of substance that wasn't quite snow or rain.

The World Cross-Country Championships, of course, have had

more than a few of those "mud fests"—which is about what you'd expect when you host them in places like Ireland, England, or Scotland.

You expect to get hills with names thrown at you. Cemetery Hill . . . Bear Cage Hill . . . Parachute Hill . . . Sure-Kill Hill . . . It all sounds appropriate, right? At its most primitive, there are still a few cross-country races out there that should actually be called "cross-water"—runners are asked to splash, or wade through, some sort of brook, creek, or river to continue on their way.

Then again, you don't necessarily expect to get knocked down by a frightened, wide-eyed deer during a race, do you? But one day I actually saw that happen to a runner from Swarthmore College as he was racing on the rural, rolling cornfield course at DeSales University in Center Valley, Pennsylvania. A herd of deer got spooked by hundreds of runners winding their way around the course and scattered across the landscape, white tails flickering in fear. Imagine getting blindsided by a deer bursting out of the cornfields when you least expect it! Never mind "the Bear" jumping on your back . . . We're talking real hooves and antlers here. To his credit, the kid got up and finished. (I probably could find out his name, with a little legwork, and use it in *Running Trivia II*.)

In addition to toughness, and a certain willingness to endure the onslaught of the elements ("Become one with the mud," advised one Lynn Jennings, a multi-time champion in the sport), tactics play a role in successful cross-country running.

There are the die-hard, lead-from-the-start "chargers," like Nick Rose—the Bristol boy who looked like he could have played for the Rolling Stones. John Treacy, the Irishman, who did so well over hill and dale in his career, had this nugget of advice: "Around a tight bend, take off like holy hell!"

Just make sure there's no terrified deer bounding toward you in the opposite direction.

1. This Ivy League college already had a Hare and Hounds Club in 1880, and a top varsity cross-country/track program headed up by distance star John Cregan in 1899. Name the college.

A. Amherst; B. Brown; C. Princeton; D. New York University

2. The first U.S. national championship in cross-country took place in:

A. 1865; B. 1890; C. 1900; D. 1915

3. Lynn Jennings won three World Cross-Country crowns racing in the U.S. vest, the third of which (coming in 1992) was especially sweet because it came after racing through the snow on this famous New England layout. Name the course and its city.

4. The famous hill on this New England course is called:

A. Ante Up Hill; B. Bear Cage Hill; C. Cemetery Hill; D. Doomsday Hill

5. Who donated the land for Kansas University's Rim Farm cross-country course, the site of numerous championship meets?

6. There are black-painted steel silhouettes of some famous Jayhawk runners perched around the course. Name three of the six runners depicted.

7. Three of these world-class milers won NCAA Division I cross-country individual titles. Which one did *not*?

A. Joe Falcon of Arkansas; B. Wes Santee of Kansas; C. Glenn Cunningham of Kansas; D. Tom O'Hara of Loyola (Illinois)

8. In addition to accomplishments on the track (he once set a world record of 8:58.4 for two miles), this former Indiana star won seven straight U.S. cross-country titles between 1934 and 1940. Name him.

A. Fred Wilt; B. Flash Perkins; C. Greg Rice; D. Don Lash

9. That record of seven straight titles was eventually eclipsed by this runner—nicknamed "the Panther"—who did his training in the thin-air, high mountains of Alamosa, Colorado. He won those eight U.S. cross-country titles from 1982 to 1989. Name him.

10. The runner who finally snapped the Panther's U.S. title streak in 1990 was this former Ivy Leaguer.

A. Pete Pfitzinger; B. Bob Kempainen; C. Craig Masback; D. Paul Gompers

11. Because foreign runners were allowed to enter the U.S. Cross-Country Championships, this Finnish Olympian (who lived many years in the U.S.A.) won the American title five times back in the 1920s. Name him.

A. Paavo Nurmi; B. Ville Ritola; C. Hannes Kolehmainen; D. Lasse Viren

12. He's the only American man to win the World Cross-Country title—in fact, he went back-to-back in 1980 and 1981.

A. Frank Shorter; B. Bill Rodgers; C. Craig Virgin; D. Pat Porter

13. One of the pioneers of women's running in the U.S.A., this woman—now a coach at Seattle-Pacific University—won the World Cross-Country title five times (1967-71).

A. Francie Larrieu-Smith; B. Julie Brown; C. Doris Brown Heritage; D. Mary Decker Slaney

14. Two of this famous Finn's gold medals came in Olympic cross-country—a sport no longer contested in the Games because numerous runners collapsed in the heat of Paris in 1924. Name the Finnish runner.

A. Paavo Nurmi; B. Ville Ritola; C. Johannes Kolehmainen; D. Lasse Viren

15. **SILVER-MEDAL QUESTION.** In Paris, this African American runner from Pittsburgh prevented a medal sweep of the Olympic cross-country event by the Finns, hanging on for third place. He also was the U.S. cross-country champ in 1921. Who was he?

16. He's the only Finnish runner to have won the World Cross-Country title, turning the trick in 1973 in Belgium.

A. Pekka Paivarinta; B. Lasse Viren; C. Juha Vaatainen; D. Kaarlo Maaninka

17. He won back-to-back World Cross-Country titles in 1978 and 1979—both on muddy courses—but the second came before his home fans in Limerick, Ireland.

A. John Treacy; B. Frank O'Mara; C. Neil Cusack; D. Eamonn Coghlan

18. She's probably better known for her New York City Marathon streak, but this woman also won five World Cross-Country titles— the first coming in 1978 at Glasgow, Scotland in thick mud.

A. Ingrid Kristiansen of Norway; B. Liz Lynch of Great Britain; C. Grete Waitz of Norway; D. Lisa Ondieki of Australia

19. She won two IAAF World Cross-Country titles (1985-86)— running barefoot for an adopted country. Name her.

20. This winner of the Boston and New York City Marathons finished second in the World Cross-Country meet in 1982, behind Mohammed Kedir of Ethiopia, racing in Rome, Italy.

A. Alberto Salazar; B. Bill Rodgers; C. Greg Meyer; D. Rob de Castella

21. When he won a bronze medal in the World Cross-Country Junior race in 2001 in Belgium, it was the first time in 20 years that an American man got to stand on the awards platform.

A. Adam Goucher; B. Jorge Torres; C. Galen Rupp; D. Dathan Ritzenhein

22. In 1981 this American junior from Florida also won a World Cross-Country bronze. He eventually made a U.S. Olympic team in the marathon.

A. Bill Reifsnyder; B. Keith Brantly; C. Mark Curp; D. Ed Eyestone

23. Four American men have won World Cross-Country Junior titles. Name any three of them.

24. Her 1992 World Cross-Country Junior title—through the snow and the muck of Boston's Franklin Park that March—helped take this runner to the next level. She eventually set records in the marathon—but also had enough speed to win the Fifth Avenue Mile.

A. Lynn Jennings of the U.S.A.; B. Sonia O'Sullivan of Ireland; C. Paula Radcliffe of Great Britain; D. Deena Drossin of the U.S.A.

25. A famous cross-country race in northern Italy (it dates back to 1933) is called the *Cinque Mulini* because it runs through five

A. Taverns; B. Barns; C. Churches; D. Mills

26. Philadelphia-area runners know that "Sure Kill" and "Parachute" are two major hills on what course?

A. Pennypacker; B. Belmont Plateau; C. Valley Forge Park; D. Brandywine

27. New Jersey runners speak reverently about "the Bowl" on this challenging course—site of the NJ "Meet of Champions."

28. Sioux Passage State Park shows runners "Manmaker Hill"— twice! Name the city and state.

A. Minneapolis, Minnesota; B. Bismarck, North Dakota; C. St. Louis, Missouri; D. Deadwood, South Dakota

29. You might think that Long Island would be relatively flat, but don't tell that to New York runners who trudge up and down "bumps" on this course called "Cardiac Hill" and "Snake Hill." Name the course.

30. You have to deal with "the Dip" on this course—twice! No wonder no high school boy has broken 16 minutes on this rugged terrain. Name the course and the state.

31. So steep is "Killer Hill" on this Cuyahoga Valley course that reportedly runners who walk can sometimes pass runners trying to run! Name the state where this race is held.

A. Florida; B. New York; C. Ohio; D. Massachusetts

32. What college team—known as "the Irish Brigade" because all five of its "scorers" hailed from the Emerald Isle—finished second to Tennessee in attempting to win the NCAA cross-country title in 1971?

A. Arkansas; B. Providence College; C. Villanova; D. East Tennessee

33. Name the Irish Brigade's top runner, the NCAA individual champ that year. (Hint: Several years later, he won the Boston Marathon.)

A. Ed Leddy; B. Mike Keogh; C. Neil Cusack; D. Dan Murphy

34. This team has won more team titles than any other in NCAA Division I women's action, including six straight between 1989 and 1994.

A. Virginia; B. Brigham Young; C. Villanova; D. Wisconsin

35. Name the man who coached that team to five of those titles.

36. He's the only coach in double figures when it comes to first-place finishes in NCAA Division I cross-country—11 and perhaps still counting.

A. Mark Wetmore; B. Bill Bowerman; C. Marty Stern; D. John McDonnell

37. A two-time Big Ten cross-country champ for Illinois in the 1960s, Coach Al Carius has led this NCAA Division III men's powerhouse to 10 national titles. Name the school.

A. Alvin Chip University; B. Bentley State; C. North Central; D. Elmhurst College

38. What famous British distance runner (at age 20) won the Southern Junior race and then—later in the same day—came back and to win the highly competitive Senior Championship?

A: Ian Stewart; B. Brendan Foster; C. Sebastian Coe; D. Dave Bedford

39. He's the only Brit to have ever won the IAAF World Cross-Country senior title, winning in 1975 in Rabat, Morocco.

A. Ian Stewart; B. Jon Brown; C. Micky Morton; D. Tim Hutchings

40. To date, he's the only man to win both the Olympic Marathon gold and a World Cross-Country title—and he won back-to-back crowns in World Cross in 1984-85.

A. John Treacy of Ireland; B. Gelindo Bordin of Italy; C. Carlos Lopes of Portugal; D. Douglas Wakiihuri of Kenya

41. Despite tripping on a steep downhill late in the race, this man got back up to win the Kinney National cross-country (now Foot Locker) race his senior year in high school in 1987. The following fall, he came back to win the NCAA Division I Cross-Country title as a freshman—the only runner to accomplish this back-to-back feat. (Hint: He also won a second NCAA title his senior year.)

A. Todd Williams; B. Bob Kennedy; C. Bob Kempainen; D. Marc Davis

42. In addition to the right name in the previous question, name three other American men who won a Foot Locker (or Kinney) title in high school and then later in their careers (they all ran for the same university) added an NCAA D-I cross-country title.

43. *Running with the Buffaloes* chronicles what college cross-country team in the midst of a challenging NCAA season?

A. Arizona; B. Bucknell; C. Colorado; D. Adams State

44. Who wrote *Running with the Buffaloes?*

45. The author was an All-American runner at what school?

A. Adams State; B. Brown; C. Colorado; D. Princeton

46. In a classic clash between two Pac-10 standouts, Henry Rono sprinted away from this defending NCAA champ to win the 1979 NCAA Division I title in 28:19.6 for 10,000 meters at Lehigh's Saucon Fields in Pennsylvania. Who was the rival he relegated to second place (and what school did he run for)?

47. This long-haired Brit from Bristol, while running for Western Kentucky University, almost stunned Steve Prefontaine in 1973 and Craig Virgin in 1975 with his charge-from-the-gun tactics before finally wilting—but he did snag victory in the 1974 NCAA Division I Cross-Country race.

A. Gordon Minty; B. Brendan Foster; C. Nick Rose; D. Tony Staynings

48. In France his 2005 IAAF World Cross-Country "double"—winning both the short- and long-course races within 24 hours—argued that this man is the greatest cross-country runner in the history of the sport. It was the fourth year in a row he achieved this incredible feat.

A. Khalid Skah of Morocco; B. Kenenisa Bekele of Ethiopia; C. Paul Tergat of Kenya; D. Daniel Koman of Kenya

49. If you combine their victories, how many World Cross-Country individual titles have Kenyan cross-country stars John Ngugi and Paul Tergat notched?

A. 6; B. 8; C. 10; D. 13

50. This Notre Dame runner won the very first NCAA cross-country race in 1938. He also was a two-time NCAA track champion in the 2-mile run.

A. Ryan Shay; B. Joe Montana; C. George Gipp; D. Greg Rice

51. Steve Prefontaine didn't win the NCAA cross-country title in his freshman year (1969), but he was only 12 seconds off the record-setting winner at Van Cortlandt Park. What place did Pre finish?

A. sixth; B. fourth; C. second; D. third

52. Racing at Wichita State in 1981, this runner was the first woman to win the NCAA Division I cross-country race.

A. Amy Skieresz of Arizona; B. Betty Jo Springs of North Carolina State; C. Angela Chalmers of Northern Arizona; D. Lesley Welch of Virginia

53. From 1938 up to (and including) 1964, the National Collegiate Cross-Country Championships were held at one site. Where?

A. Indiana University in Bloomington; B. the University of Wisconsin in Madison; C. Michigan State University in East Lansing; D. the University of Kansas in Lawrence

54. The distance the men raced from 1938 to 1964 was:

A. 2.5 miles; B. 3 miles; C. 3.5 miles; D. 4 miles

55. **SILVER-MEDAL QUESTION.** Only three men have won three NCAA cross-country titles. Name them.

56. **GOLD-MEDAL QUESTION.** Only one woman—a Division III runner from Wartburg in Iowa (and also a two-time qualifier for the U.S. World Cross-Country team)—has won three NCAA

Cross-Country titles. Name her.

57. She's got the fastest Foot Locker time ever posted, with 16:24.

A. Amber Trotter; B. Erin Keogh; C. Connie Robinson; D. Melody Fairchild

58. He's got the fastest Foot Locker time ever posted, clocking 14:29.

A. Adam Goucher; B. Bob Kennedy; C. Marc Davis; D. Dathan Ritzenhein

59. True or False. As of 2004, no female Foot Locker (Kinney) cross-country champ has been able to go on and win an NCAA Division I cross country title.

60. There have been five (counting both genders) "double winners" in the Foot Locker (Kinney) Cross-Country Championships, who won the race twice in their high school careers. List three of the five.

61. This famous New York City cross-country course is one of the oldest in America and served as the 1968 and 1969 NCAA Championships. It is:

A: Central Park; B. Battery Park; C. Van Cortlandt Park; D. Riverside Park

62. This famous and scenic course in San Diego often serves as the home site of the Foot Locker Cross-Country Championship—a race among the best 32 high school runners in the country.

A. Pizarro Park; B. Balboa Park; C. Cortes Park; D. Del Coronado Park

63. Despite all their distance-running history on the track (and four NCAA team championships in cross-country), only one Villanova Wildcat runner can claim an NCAA individual men's title in cross-country. Name him.

A. Sydney Maree; B. Vic Zwolak; C. Eamonn Coghlan; D. Donal Walsh

64. With seven crowns, this team leads the pack in NCAA Division I women's team titles.

A. Virginia; B. North Carolina State; C. Colorado; D. Villanova

65. True or False. The University of Wisconsin women have won more Big Ten cross-country crowns than the rest of the conference teams combined.

66. Only three Big Ten runners—all Olympic-caliber runners—have won the individual conference title four times. Name them and their schools.

67. Led by two-time individual champ Ralph Serna and future world-class miler Steve Scott, this team won the NCAA Division II cross-country title in 1975 and 1976 under the direction of Coach Len Miller.

A. Arizona State; B. Pacific University; C. the University of California-Irvine; D. San Diego State

68. **BRONZE-MEDAL QUESTION.** Name the U.S. president who attended one of the military academies and ran cross-country there.

69. He's the only runner from one of the military academies to win the NCAA individual cross-country title—and the following year, he finished second to a Washington State star.

A. Mike Ryan, U.S. Air Force Academy; B. Dan Browne, U.S. Military Academy; C. Ronnie Harris, U.S. Naval Academy; D. Dick Shea, U.S. Military Academy

70. GOLD-MEDAL QUESTION. Name the pilot of the space shuttle *Columbia*—a former U.S. Naval Academy cross-country captain—who perished in the tragic reentry into the Earth's atmosphere of that craft on February 1, 2003. His teammates honored him by dedicating a modest memorial on the Naval Academy cross-country course.

71. BRONZE-MEDAL QUESTION. In 1994 this son of an Olympic champion won the NCAA Division I individual title for the University of Arizona. Name him.

72. Only two coaches in the history of NCAA Division I cross-country competition have coached national championship teams for both genders. Name them.

73. How many U.S. Cross-Country titles did Lynn Jennings win in her stellar career?

A. two; B. four; C. six; D. nine

74. Running as a collegiate for Princeton, how many NCAA cross-country titles did Lynn Jennings win?

A. zero; B. one; C. two; D. three

75. What European runner (circa 1970s) finished second three straight times in the World Cross-Country Championships? (Hint: He also had some hard luck on the track, placing fourth—one out of the medals—in the Olympic 10,000 in 1972.)

A. Anthony Simmons of Great Britain; B. Marc Smet of Belgium; C. Alberto Cova of Italy; D. Mariano Haro Cisneros of Spain

76. In the 1990s this Irish runner had to settle for four straight World Cross-Country silver medals. (Hint: She also ran well in the half-marathon and marathon events.) Name her.

77. In 1998 she won both the 8-K senior women's race and the short course 4-K at Marrakech, Morocco. In college she won two NCAA cross-country titles for powerhouse Villanova.

A. Vicki Huber of the U.S.A.; B. Sonia O'Sullivan of Ireland; C. Carole Zajac of the U.S.A.; D. Carrie Tollefson of the U.S.A.

78. In NCAA Division II women's cross-country, two teams have accounted for 18 team titles between them between 1981 and 2004. Name those two teams.

79. What brother-sister team can both claim to having won a pair of U.S. cross-country titles—the brother in the mid-1960s and his sister in the 1970s? They both also made the U.S. Olympic track team.

80. This New York runner showed his great range, winning a silver medal in the 1912 Olympic 1500—but then winning the U.S. Cross-Country crown the next year. Later in life he also ran a leg on the Olympic torch relay. Name this gutsy little runner.

81. As a two-time World Cross-Country champ, Khalid Skah of Morocco proved he could give the Kenyans and Ethiopians a run for their money. What does *Skah* translate (roughly) to in Arabic?

A. tough mind; B. speed; C. runaway; D. duel

82. Colleen De Reuck has won the last two U.S. cross-country long-course races and won the 2004 U.S. Olympic Marathon Trials. In her first major race in a U.S.A. singlet, De Reuck placed third overall and helped lead the Americans to a silver medal in the 2002 World Cross-Country finish in Dublin. What country did she run for prior to changing her citizenship?

A. South Africa; B. Great Britain; C. Germany; D. the Netherlands

83. This famous American runner credits his third place in the 1975 World Cross-Country Championships as the confidence booster and springboard to his first big marathon breakthrough the next month.

A. Alberto Salazar; B. Bill Rodgers; C. Craig Virgin; D. Dick Beardsley

84. This South African, representing Indiana, won the women's NCAA Division I cross-country title in 1989—running barefoot! Name her.

A. Elana Meyer; B. Zola Budd; C. Frith van der Merwe; D. Michelle Dekkers

85. In 2004 this eye-opening high school team placed four young women in the Foot Locker Nationals with a stunning performance at the Northeast Regional Meet at Van Cortlandt Park in New York. Name this New York high school.

86. Nicole Blood, the leader of this impressive pack, also did something during the season that no other high school girl had achieved at Van Cortlandt Park, cranking out this course record time for the 2.5-mile layout.

A. under 15 minutes; B. under 14:30; C. under 14 minutes; D. under 13:30

87. Although he's definitely better known for the mile, Alan Webb can also run well in cross-country. What place did he finish in the Foot Locker Nationals his senior year in high school?

A. first; B. second; C. third; D; seventh

88. Webb's college career was extremely short, since he went "pro" after his freshman year. What honors—if any—did he win in collegiate cross-country competition?

89. York High School in Elmhurst puts claim to 19 national titles and 24 Illinois state crowns. Name the coach of this team.

90. The title of one of this coach's books alludes to the color of the school uniforms and the depth of the York team. Name the book.

91. This cross-country meet in North Carolina—with high school and college divisions—brings together some of the most impressive preps to race against each other. What is the meet called?

CROSS-COUNTRY
ANSWERS

1. C
2. B
3. Franklin Park in Boston
4. B
5. Bob Timmons, who coached Jim Ryun in high school and at Kansas
6. Jim Ryun, Wes Santee, Billy Mills, Johnny Lawson, Herb Semper, and Al Frame
7. C
8. D
9. Pat Porter
10. B
11. B
12. C
13. C
14. A
15. Earle Johnson
16. A
17. A
18. C

19. Zola Budd—who had switched her South African citizenship to British
20. A
21. D
22. B
23. Rich Kimball, Bob Thomas, Eric Hulst, Thom Hunt
24. C
25. D
26. B
27. Holmdel Park
28. C
29. Sunken Meadow
30. Hereford, Maryland
31. C
32. D
33. C
34. C
35. Marty Stern
36. D
37. C
38. D
39. A
40. C
41. B
42. Adam Goucher, Jorge Torres, Dathan Ritzenhein
43. C
44. Chris Lear
45. D
46. Alberto Salazar of Oregon
47. C

48. B

49. C

50. D

51. D

52. B

53. C

54. D

55. Gerry Lindgren (Washington State, 1966-67, 1969); Steve Prefontaine (Oregon, 1970-71, 1973); Henry Rono (Washington State, 1976-77, 1979)

56. Missy Buttry

57. A

58. D

59. True

60. Melody Fairchild, Dathan Ritzenhein, Erin Keogh, Erin Sullivan, Abdirizak Mohamud

61. C

62. B

63. B

64. D

65. True. As of 2004, the Badgers have 13 Big Ten titles.

66. Craig Virgin of Illinois, Bob Kennedy of Indiana, and Kevin Sullivan of Michigan (by way of Canada).

67. A

68. Jimmy Carter

69. A

70. William "Willy" McCool, who graduated second in his class and went on to become an accomplished test pilot before the ill-fated *Columbia* mission.

71. Martin Keino, son of Kip Keino

72. Martin Smith: Virginia (women 1982), Wisconsin (men, 1985, 1988); and Mark Wetmore: Colorado (women, 2004), Colorado (men, 2001, 2004)

73. D

74. A

75. D

76. Catherina McKiernan of Ireland

77. B

78. Adams State with 10, and Cal Poly-San Luis Obispo with 8

79. Ron Larrieu and Francie Larrieu-Smith

80. Abel Kiviat

81. C

82. A

83. B

84. D

85. Saratoga Springs

86. C. Blood ran 13:57.

87. B

88. He was Big Ten champ and he also made All-American in the NCAA D-I national race, with his 11th-place finish.

89. Joe Newton

90. *The Long Green Line*

91. The Great American Cross-Country Festival

SPRINTS, LONG SPRINTS, AND HURDLES

When I was putting together *The Quotable Runner* about a decade ago, I didn't include the sprinters (with very few exceptions), just because I was primarily focused on the middle- and long-distance runners—and that bunch (probably because they have a lot of time to think) had more than enough to say.

Sprinters and hurdlers, on the other hand, shoot from the hip (or, verbally, from "the lip")—athletes who live and die by their quick reactions. There's just not a whole lot of leisurely contemplation going on there. Along that line of thought, 1920s sprint coach Sam Mussabini once advised: "Only think of two things—the report of the pistol and the tape. When you hear the one, just run like hell till you break the other."

But this project allowed me to include a virtual treasure chest of trivia from the fast-twitch world, including one of my favorite questions in the entire book—specifically, name the sprinter whom eccentric owner Charlie Finley hired to pinch-run for the Oakland Athletics in the 1970s. One of the reasons I like that particular question is that I woke up in the middle of the night and, for some strange reason, remembered the sprinter's name. Baseball enthusiasts, one should think, will have a leg up on that particular question. (And if you're *really* sharp, how does former

Los Angeles Dodger hurler Mike Marshall figure into it all?)

Working on the sprint section also helped me rapidly dispatch a recent *Jeopardy* quiz question—the question with the best "pay-off" in the category, in fact. The category had something to do with gloves; and the answer had something to do with two extremely fast American sprinters from the late 1960s. I don't want to give too much away on that one, for what should be an obvious reason.

Offered as "a section within a section," the 800-meter types frequently present a classification dilemma for track-and-field buffs. Is it a middle-distance event or a long sprint? Rate of speed might figure into the formula—a novice runner trying to break 2:10 for the first time is one thing; but world-class runners blitzing through the 400-meter split in 50-flat are cheetahs with quite different spots.

There's an old argument, though, that suggests that sprinters are born, not made. Certainly this is more true for 100-meter sprinters than it is for 800-meter runners. Jesse Owens, even without any real training, was still able to clock a 9.8 100-yard dash at age 43—some 20 years after his heyday.

I learned early on, running the 75-yard dash in junior high school, that my future wasn't going to have much to do with starting blocks. Still, you couldn't help love the *sounds* of sprinting—the churning of spikes in real cinders (I'm going back in time now, I confess), the audible *puff-puff-puff* of the speedster churning through the turn. . . the slap of the baton in the anchorman's hand . . . the words "Go! Go! *Go!*" chasing him down the homestretch.

As for the rest of us, there's always the marathon . . .

1. What famous sprint star's running form was once aptly described by Simon Barnes of the London *Times* as "Groucho Marx chasing a waitress"?

A. Jesse Owens; B. Butch Reynolds; C. Carl Lewis; D. Michael Johnson

2. Jeremy Wariner's 43.93 clocking for the 400-meter gold medal at the 2005 Worlds in Helsinki made him only the eighth runner in history to crack the magical 44-second barrier. Of all the runners who have ever gone under 44 seconds in that event, how many are Americans?

A. All eight; B. six; C. four; D. three

3. What former sprint great became Jeremy Wariner's agent?

A. Alonzo Babers; B. John Smith; C. Carl Lewis; D. Michael Johnson

4. Edwin Moses, the greatest 400-meter hurdler in history, stretched his win streak in that event to what number?

A. 88; B. 101; C. 107; D. 133

5. The last man to defeat Moses before he began his famous streak was:

A. Harald Schmid of West Germany; B. John Akii-Bua of Uganda; C. Ralph Mann of the U.S.A.; D. David Hemery of Great Britain

6. The hurdler who finally snapped Moses's streak was:

A. Andre Phillips of the U.S.A.; B. Volker Beck of East Germany; C. Harald Schmid of West Germany; D. Danny Harris of the U.S.A.

7. Moses's streak lasted how many days?

A. 333; B. 555; C. 666; D. 999

8. In the 1988 Games in Seoul, Moses placed:

A. second; B. third; C. eighth; D. fourth in his semi-final heat

9. This University of Kansas athlete won an NCAA 400-meter title and finished second in the 1960 Rome Olympics behind an American teammate. In 1964 he hit a hurdle, and that cost him a chance on another U.S. Olympic squad. An air force fighter pilot, he remains officially "missing in action" in the Vietnam War. Name him.

10. Two Olympic gold medals (100 meters) and three world titles (100-meter hurdles) arguably make her the best ever sprint/hurdle athlete in women's track. But perhaps her biggest hurdle was overcoming Graves' disease—a thyroid illness that, before it was properly diagnosed, almost led to amputation of her feet. Name her.

11. BRONZE-MEDAL QUESTION. In 1932 Bob Tisdall won the Olympic gold medal for Ireland in the 400-meter hurdles in 51.7 seconds. Silver medalist Glenn Hardin of the U.S.A. ran 51.9. Both men broke the world record of 52.0-flat, but Hardin—the runner-up—was credited for the world record. Why?

12. Nazi leader Adolf Hitler allegedly invited her to spend the weekend at his summer retreat in Berchtesgaden after she won the women's 100-meter race at Berlin in 1936. She rebuffed the Fuehrer's overtures.

A. Stella Walsh of Poland; B. Fanny Blankers-Koen of the Netherlands; C. Hilde Strike of Canada; D. Helen Stephens of the U.S.A.

13. At the Amsterdam Olympics, this sprinter became the first woman to ever win an Olympic gold medal. She tied her own world record of 12.2 in the 100 meters. She also won relay medals in Amsterdam and Berlin.

A. Fanny Blankers-Koen of the Netherlands; B. Betty Robinson of the U.S.A.; C. Ethel Smith of Canada; D. Hilde Strike of Canada

14. A street in Berlin is named after this Olympic star.

A. Armin Hary of West Germany; B. Rudolf Harbig of Germany; C. Jesse Owens of the U.S.A.; D. Lutz Long of Germany

15. Name the only man to win back-to-back gold medals in consecutive Olympic Games in the men's 400-meter hurdles.

A. John Akii-Bua of Uganda; B. Glenn Hardin of the U.S.A.; C. Edwin Moses of the U.S.A.; D. Glenn Davis of the U.S.A.

16. Southern Cal ran a world record 38.6 for the 4 x 110-yard (440-yard relay) in 1967 when the Trojans won that event at the NCAA Championships. It was anchored by this late two-time Olympic sprint medal winner from Jamaica, which meant it couldn't count as an American record.

A. Michael Fray; B. Lennox Miller; C. Hasely Crawford; D. Don Quarie

17. This infamous "celebrity" ran a leg on that record-setting relay. But his most famous runs took place on the football field, and, later in life, a "run" in a Ford Bronco. Name him.

18. Long before this athlete was placed on the 23-cent stamp, his/her stick-to-it-iveness was proved by overcoming various childhood illnesses, including polio—going on to win three gold sprint medals in Rome.

A. Wilma Rudolph of the U.S.A.; B. Fanny Blankers-Koen of the Netherlands; C. Charley Paddock of the U.S.A.; D. Harrison Dillard of the U.S.A.

19. This sprinter was the first athlete to win back-to-back 100-meter Olympic titles.

A. Wyomia Tyus of the U.S.A.; B. Valery Borzov of the Soviet Union; C. Jesse Owens of the U.S.A.; D. Wilma Rudolph of the U.S.A.

20. She's the only U.S. woman to win two U.S. Olympic Trial 100-meter-dash crowns.

A. Evelyn Ashford; B. Gwen Torrence; C. Florence Griffith Joyner; D. Marion Jones

21. **GOLD-MEDAL QUESTION.** Name the national-class sprinter—four-time All-American, seven Big Ten titles—that appeared in 104 Major League Baseball games for the Oakland Athletics in the mid-1970s, but only as a "designated runner."

22. This hired sprint gun stole 31 bases and scored 33 runs in his MLB career. His most memorable World Series moment came against the Los Angeles Dodgers when:

A. he stole home plate; B. he scored from first on a long single to right field; C. he was caught in a rundown and tagged out; D. he was quickly picked off at first base

23. Jesse Owens cranked out an Olympic-record 20.6 to strike gold in the 1936 Berlin Olympics. Teammate Mack Robinson supported with a silver-medal race behind Owens, but the most famous athlete in Robinson's family was his younger brother. Name that baseball player.

A. Jackie Robinson of the Brooklyn Dodgers; B. Brooks Robinson of the Baltimore Orioles; C. Frank Robinson of the Cincinnati Reds and Baltimore Orioles

24. Name the only two 110-meter hurdlers in history to have successfully defended their Olympic titles.

A. Renaldo Nehemiah and Greg Foster of the U.S.A.; B. Edwin

Moses and Renaldo Nehemiah of the U.S.A.; C. Lee Calhoun and Roger Kingdom of the U.S.A.; D. Guy Drut of France and Willie Davenport of the U.S.A.

25. Showing amazing sprint range, this woman won Olympic gold medals in the 100, 200, and 400 meters during her career—but the 400 win (an Olympic record at the time) came eight years after the short-sprint victories.

A. Marita Koch of East Germany; B. Fanny Blankers-Koen of the Netherlands; C. Betty Cuthbert of Australia; D. Florence Griffith Joyner of the U.S.A.

26. In 1948 the "flying housewife" won four of the nine events on the Olympic track-and-field schedule for women. In her honor, there is a track meet named for her and a running statue in her likeness.

A: Fanny Blankers-Koen of the Netherlands; B. Babe Didriksen of the U.S.A.; C. Betty Cuthbert of Australia; D. Yvette Williams of New Zealand

27. Born Stanislawa Walasiewiczowna in Poland, this runner set world records in the sprints (60 meters, 100 meters, 200 meters, 220 yards) in the mid-1930s. But when she died of gunshot wounds, the subsequent autopsy showed "she" had male sex organs. Give the name this athlete raced under in competition.

28. Name the two black American 200-meter sprinters who participated in the infamous "black power" victory stand protest at the Mexico City Olympic Games in 1968.

29. This Australian sprinter, the silver-medal winner, was the third man on the victory stand during that 1968 protest—but his accomplishment was arguably upstaged by the political controversy.

A. Rupert Murdoch; B. Nigel Barker; C. Russell Crowe; D. Peter Norman

30. He's the only man to ever with both the 400- and 200-meter Olympic races and the only man to also successfully defend an Olympic 400 meter crown.

A. Jesse Owens of the U.S.A.; B. Butch Reynolds of the U.S.A.; C. Michael Johnson of the U.S.A; D. Eric Liddell of Great Britain

31. True or False. Olympic hurdling great Glenn Davis also was a standout football player, teaming with the legendary "Doc" Blanchard in the West Point backfield.

32. This top-notch sprinter from USC ran on three world record-

setting and Olympic gold-medal-winning 4 x 100 relay teams—
Amsterdam, Los Angeles, and Berlin—accomplishments that no
doubt helped offset two fourth place Olympic finishes in the 100
meters.

A. Earl Vickery; B. Frank Wykoff; C. Charley Paddock; D. Victor
Williams

33. All four of these fantastic 110-meter hurdle stars held the world
record (or shared the WR) in their event at one time or another. But
which one never won an Olympic medal?

A. Renaldo Nehemiah of the U.S.A.; B. Willie Davenport of the
U.S.A.; C. Lee Calhoun of the U.S.A.; D. Guy Drut of France

34. Which one of these world-class hurdlers also participated in the
1980 Winter Olympic Games in the four-man bobsled event?

A. Renaldo Nehemiah; B. Rod Milburn; C. Roger Kingdom; D.
Willie Davenport

35. He ruled the 110-meter hurdles in the 1980s—not only winning Olympic gold medals in both 1984 and 1988, but also twice
setting Olympic records in the process.

A. Greg Foster of the U.S.A.; B. Renaldo Nehemiah of the U.S.A.;
C. Colin Jackson of Great Britain; D. Roger Kingdom of the U.S.A.

36. Name the American hurdler who won the world championship 110-meter hurdle title in five straight IAAF Championship meets until he finally settled for a bronze in Helsinki in 2005.

37. How high are the men's 110-meter hurdles?

A. 4 feet; B. 3 feet, 3 inches; C. 3 feet, 6 inches; D. 4 feet, 4 inches

38. How many hurdles must the runners get over in the 400-meter hurdle event?

A. six; B. eight; C. ten; D. twelve

39. These pioneers of track from the University of Pennsylvania claimed gold medals in the 110-meter and 400-meter hurdles, respectively, at the 1900 Paris Olympic Games. Name them.

40. What was used for hurdles in the 1900 Paris Olympic Games?

A. hay bales; B. bricks; C. large logs; D. telephone poles

41. When she won the 400-meter hurdles (an inaugural event for women) at the 1984 Olympic Games, the king in her country stat-

ed that all the girls born on that day should be named in her honor.

A. Hassiba Boulmerka of Algeria; B. Nawal El Moutawakel of Morocco; C. Cristina Cojocaru of Romania; D. Yordanka Donkova of Bulgaria

42. He was the first man to break 50 seconds in the 400-meter hurdles.

A. Glenn Hardin of the U.S.A.; B. Bob Tisdall of Ireland; C. Rex Cawley of the U.S.A.; D. Glenn Davis of the U.S.A.

43. Which of these British Olympic sprint champions was nicknamed "the Beast" for his powerful physique?

A. Harold Abrahams; B. Allan Wells; C. Linford Christie; D. Eric Liddell

44. The 1952 Olympic men's 100-meter final was so close that the first four men were all hand-timed in 10.4 on Helsinki's muddy track. It took officials 20 minutes of studying still photos to confirm that this man—despite starting his finish-line lean too early—won the race.

A. Lindy Remigino of the U.S.A.; B. Bob Hayes of the U.S.A.; C. Herbert McKenley of Jamaica; D. Dean Smith of the U.S.A.

45. He was the first man to break 47 seconds in the 400-meter hurdles.

A. John Akii-Bua of Uganda; B. Edwin Moses of the U.S.A.; C. Kevin Young of the U.S.A.; D. Danny Harris of the U.S.A.

46. In 1968 this man twice broke 10 seconds for the 100-meter sprint (the first man to do it), once hand-timed and once electronically timed. Set at altitude, his electronic mark of 9.95 stood for nearly 15 years. Name this sprinter.

A. Archie Hahn of the U.S.A.; B. Bob Hayes of the U.S.A.; C. Jim Hines of the U.S.A.; D. Valery Borzov of the Soviet Union

47. Jesse Owens's first name at birth was:

A. James; B. Jessup; C. Charles; D. Dellwood

48. Owens's nickname was:

A. "Alabama Lightning"; B. "The Buckeye Bullet"; C. "Quicksilver"; D. "The Golden Blur"

49. At age 13, this future Olympic great received inspiration-plus when the great Jesse Owens presented him with a pair of running shoes. Who was this American star—the only man to ever win gold medals in the Olympic 100 meters *and* the Olympic 110-meter hurdles?

A. Barney Ewell; B. Bob Joe Morrow; C. Charlie Greene; D. Harrison Dillard

50. Because of his lanky build, this American sprint star was nicknamed "Bones."

A. Willie Gault; B. Bob Hayes; C. Carl Lewis; D. Harrison Dillard

51. This Italian sprinter competed in four straight Olympiads, won the 200-meter gold in Moscow in 1980, and broke Tommie Smith's 11-year-old WR with 19:72 at Mexico City in 1979.

A. Michael Agostini; B. Livio Berruti; C. Luigi Beccali; D. Pietro Mennea

52. This Soviet sprint champ captured both the 100- and 200-meter races at the 1972 Munich Games. Name him.

53. This 1964 100-meter gold-medal winner equaled the world record with his 10-flat at Tokyo. But later some of his sprints involved running fly patterns for the Dallas Cowboys.

A. Herschel Walker; B. Bob Hayes; C. Gayle Sayers; D. Glenn Davis

54. Two men considered medal contenders at Munich in the 100 meters never made the final. Name the two U.S. sprinters who missed their semifinal heat because of a change in the scheduling.

55. After rushing to compete in his semifinal heat, this American did finish second to the Soviet runner—and second to him again in the final.

A. Jim Hines; B. Robert Taylor; C. Charlie Greene; D. Sam Grady

56. Fewer than half a dozen non-American sprinters have ever held the men's world record for the 100-meter dash. Name three of them.

57. Harold Abrahams won the 1924 100-meter race—something of an upset—that was immortalized in the award-winning film *Chariots of Fire.* Name the American 100-meter world record holder and defending Olympic champ whom Abrahams beat in that event.

A. Jackson Scholz; B. Chester Bowman; C. Charley Paddock; D. Ralph Metcalfe

58. Despite racing in the outside lane, this man ran a blistering first 200 meters en route to an Olympic-record 47.6 at the 1924 Paris Games.

A. Horatio Fitch of the U.S.A.; B. Bevil Rudd of South Africa; C. Charley Paddock of the U.S.A.; D. Eric Liddell of Great Britain

59. Despite drawing the first lane (considered a disadvantage in the 400-meter hurdles), this man raced to a world and Olympic record (47.82), plus defeated the defending Olympic champ at Munich in 1972.

A. John Akii-Bua of Uganda; B. Volker Beck of East Germany; C. Edwin Moses of the U.S.A.; D. David Hemery of Great Britain

60. His disqualification for banned substances moved Carl Lewis—the defending champ from Los Angeles—up to the gold in the 1988 Seoul Olympic Games in the 100 meters. Name him.

61. Although American runners have historically dominated the men's 400-meter dash at the Olympic Games, this country blasted to back-to-back 1-2 finishes in that event in 1948 and 1952.

A. Jamaica; B. Great Britain; C. Cuba; D. Soviet Union

62. Bonus: Name the 1948 and 1952 men's 400-meter winners from the above country.

63. The same man—a fellow countryman—won the silver behind the above winners. He was also the first man to break 46 seconds for the 400-meter dash.

A: Herbert McKenley; B. Bob Marley; C. Raymond Stewart; D. Lenox Miller

64. The German women were heavily favored to win the 4 x 100-meter relay in the 1936 Olympic Games in Berlin. But when they dropped the baton—with a big lead—on the final pass, the U.S. scooted home first. Adolf Hitler called the German women to his Olympic booth and:

A. awarded them their own medals; B. berated them for the mistake; C. consoled them for their bad luck; D. offered them champagne to calm them down

65. This American 4 x 100 relay team—including the great Jesse Owens—was the first ever to crack the 40-second barrier, with 39.8 in the Berlin Olympic Games, relegating Italy and Germany to a distant battle for silver and bronze. Name any of the other team members of that 1936 team.

66. Their world record in this event lasted for:

A. 10 years; B. 12 years; C. 17 years; D. 20 years

67. The relay selection was controversial because two Jewish athletes were removed from the quartet. Name them.

68. The current women's world record for the 4 x 100-meter relay—a smoking 41.37—was set by the German Democratic Republic. Approximately how long (as of 2005) has that record stood?

A. 10 years; B. 20 years; C. 25 years; D. 29 years

69. In the 60-meter indoor dash, this woman has the five fastest times ever clocked—including the women's world record at 6.92. Name her.

A. Irina Privalova of Russia; B. Merlene Ottey of Jamaica.; C. Marion Jones of the U.S.A.; D. Gail Devers of the U.S.A.; E. Ekaterini Thanou of Greece

70. These two women—a Bulgarian (who currently has the world record of 12.21) and a Russian (who later competed in the 1996 Olympic Games for her adopted country of Sweden)—account for 9 of the 10 fastest times ever run in the women's 100-meter hurdles.

71. True or False. Teams from the United States hold 8 of the top 10 men's 4 x 100-meter relay times ever clocked.

72. A blazing anchor leg from this multi-time Olympic medalist solidified the world record 4 x 100 of 37.40 at the Barcelona Olympic Games in 1992. Mike Marsh, Leroy Burrell, and Dennis Mitchell ran the first three legs. Name him.

73. That record was tied a year later by another U.S. quartet racing in Stuttgart, Germany. Two men ran on *both* of the teams. Name them.

74. He's the only sprinter to ever crack 6.40 seconds in the 60-meter dash.

A. Carl Lewis of the U.S.A.; B. Bruny Surin of Canada; C. Andre Cason of the U.S.A.; D. Maurice Greene of the U.S.A.

75. This Jamaican-born Olympic sprint champ didn't begin his running career until he was 24 years old—preferring the disco dance scene. He was no stranger to the spotlight.

A. Asafa Powell of Jamaica; B. Donavan Bailey of Canada; C. Linford Christie of Great Britain; D. Don Quarrie of Jamaica

76. He won the 400-meter dash at the Barcelona Olympic Games in 1992, setting an Olympic record of 43.50.

A. Steve Lewis of the U.S.A.; B. Butch Reynolds of the U.S.A; C. Quincy Watts of the U.S.A.; D. Samson Kitur of Kenya

77. After suffering a badly pulled right hamstring in a semifinal heat of the 400 meters in Barcelona, this man inspired both stadium fans and a worldwide audience when—with the help of his father—he limped home "just to finish."

A. Roger Black of Great Britain; B. Bruny Surin of Canada; C. Linford Christie of Great Britain; D. Derek Redmond of Great Britain

78. When she won the 200-meter dash in the 2005 World Championships in Helsinki, what else was noteworthy about Southern Cal student Allyson Felix's come-from-behind home-stretch victory in 22.16?

A. She tied the American record; B. Just 19, she became the youngest runner to ever win the world 200-meter title; C. She set a record for the World Championships; D. She fell coming out of the blocks, but still won

79. True or False. Allyson Felix never won an NCAA sprint title.

80. With an Olympic 100-meter gold in Athens, followed by a gold medal in the 2005 World Championship 100-meter race, Justin Gatlin joined a fairly exclusive club. Only four other men have simultaneously held both Olympic and world titles. Name three of them.

81. Critics in the Australian media dubbed her "the Greta Garbo" of track and field after this French star—a gold-medal winner in two events in Atlanta—suddenly fled the Sydney Olympic Games in 1996. In her glory days, the French media called her "Le Gazelle." Name her.

82. With the French runner out of the competition, this Australian star—and Olympic torchbearer—cruised to victory in the 400 meters at Sydney, much to the delight of the home fans.

A. Cathy Freeman; B. Lauren Hewitt; C. Betty Cuthbert; D. Lisa Martin

83. The key to fast sprinting was "relaxed jaw muscles" according to this devout Christian sprinter. He was an NCAA champ in the 100 and 200, won both those events in the Olympics, plus anchored his 4 x 100 to world-record gold—all in 1956.

A. Eric Liddell of Great Britain; B. Bobby Joe Morrow of the U.S.A.; C. Paul Pilgrim of the U.S.A.; D. Forrest Smithson

84. True or False. The U.S.A. has not won a men's 4 x 100 or 4 x 400-meter relay in Pan American Games competition since 1987, when the meet was hosted in Indianapolis.

85. This English lord held off two Americans in the 400-meter hurdles to land the gold medal at Amsterdam in 1928. In 1931, he had to request a leave of absence from the British Parliament to compete in Los Angeles the next year.

A. Albert Hall; B. David Burghley; C. Thomas Livingstone-Learmonth; D. F. Morgan Taylor

86. Just 18 years old, this man had been running the 400-meter hurdles in competition for less than five months when he finished second to Edwin Moses in the Olympic Games.

A. Amadou Ba of Senegal; B. Volker Beck of East Germany; C. Mike Shine of the U.S.A.; D. Danny Harris of the U.S.A.

87. Cuban Olympic star Alberto Juantorena competed in both the 400 (twice) and 800 (once) events in Pan American competition (in 1975 and 1979). How many gold medals did he win in those individual Pan American events?

A. three; B. two; C. one; D. none

88. Spanish 101. Cuban stud Alberto Juantorena's nickname was "El Caballo." In Spanish that means:

A. The Animal; B. The Bullet; C. The Cannibal; D. The Horse

89. Backed up by what was probably a posed or doctored picture, a persistent story goes that this man won the 1908 Olympic 120-yard hurdles while carrying a Bible in his hand—allegedly as a protest for races being run on Sundays.

A. Eric Liddell of Great Britain; B. Bobby Joe Morrow of the U.S.A.; C. Forrest Smithson of the U.S.A.; D. Tracy Smith of the U.S.A.

90. Running on the 4 x 400-meter relay in London in 1908, this University of Pennsylvania runner became the first black Olympian to win a gold medal.

91. What famous World War II general once ran the 200-meter hurdles competitively for West Point? (Hint: He also competed in the 1912 Olympic Games in the military pentathlon event)

A. Douglas MacArthur; B. Omar Bradley; C. George S. Patton; D. Dwight Eisenhower

92. When his father, William, died in 1987, this great Olympic sprinter placed a gold medal from the 1984 Games in the coffin with him.

A. Rod Milburn; B. Bob Hayes; C. Carl Lewis; D. Calvin Smith

THE 800 METER MEN

93. "I am very satisfied for now . . . Please don't ask me about breaking 1:40!" implored this man to the press after running 1:41.11—the world record for 800 meters.

A. Haile Gebrselassie of Ethiopia; B. Vebjorn Rodal of Norway; C. Noah Ngeny of Kenya; D. Wilson Kipketer of Denmark

94. The previous world-record holder for 800 meters had held the honor for 16 years. Name him.

A. Alberto Juantorena of Cuba; B. Joaquim Cruz of Brazil; C. Sebastian Coe of Great Britain; D. Steve Ovett of Great Britain

95. A 1:49 leg was the *slow* split on this world record-setting 4 x 800-meter relay team from Great Britain and Northern Ireland that clocked 7:03.89 in London in 1982. Name any three of the four runners on that team.

96. In Stuttgart, Germany, in 1999, two teams came close to the British/NI record, with South Africa's anchor man Johan Botha needing a 1:44.3 leg to hold off a Kenyan contingent from this school. The South Africans ran 7:04.70 . . . less than two-tenths of a second ahead of the Kenyans.

A. Nairobi University, Kenya; B. Washington State; C. The University of Texas-El Paso; D. St. Patrick's School, Kenya

97. GOLD-MEDAL QUESTION. In the 1928 Olympic Games in Amsterdam, Lina Radke of Germany lowered her own 800-meter record by nearly 3 seconds—clocking 2:16.8 to win the gold. What else was significant about that 800-meter race?

98. After lackluster performances in her trial and semifinal 800-meter heat, this runner strongly considered skipping the 1964 Tokyo Olympic final to go shopping. It was a good thing she didn't, since she won gold and set what was then an Olympic record of 2:01.1. Who was she?

A. Ann Packer of Great Britain; B. Lyudmila Shevtsova of the Soviet Union; C. Betty Cuthbert of Australia; D. Maryvonne Dupureur of France

99. In 1985 this enduring veteran set the U.S. men's record for 800 meters with 1:42.60—and seven years later at Barcelona he landed an Olympic bronze in the two-lap.

A. Johnny Gray; B. Mark Everett; C. Jose Parrilla; D. Earl Jones

100. In 1939 this German runner simultaneously held the world record in both the 400- and 800-meter races. He was killed in

action on the Russian front in 1944, and the sports stadium in Dresden—the city of his birth—was renamed in his honor in 1951.

A. Lutz Long; B. Olaf Beyer; C. Rudolf Harbig; D. Dr. Otto Peltzer

101. "My hat made it into the Track & Field Hall of Fame before I did!" this American Olympic 800 champion quipped. But he was embarrassed when he forgot to take off that same hat at the 1972 medal ceremony.

A. Mel Sheppard; B. Ted Meredith; C. Tom Courtney; D. Dave Wottle

102. The silver medalist (a unanimous pick to win in the *Track & Field News* preview), who led most of the gun lap but lost to the above runner—despite a finish-line dive—said: "It's very disappointing to lose in the last stride by the length of your nose."

A. Yevgeny Arzhanov of the Soviet Union; B. Mike Boit of Kenya; C. Franz-Joseph Kemper of West Germany; D. Ivo van Damme of Belgium

103. This man passed Kenya's Wilson Kiprugut in the final meters of the 800-meter run and equaled the world record for 800 meters (1:44.3) to win the gold medal at Mexico City in 1968.

A. Peter Snell of New Zealand; B. Mike Boit of Kenya; C. Bill Crothers of Canada; D. Ralph Doubell of Australia

104. In a classic 800-meter duel, this woman held off defending champion Meredith Rainey to win the 1990 NCAA Division I two-lap title. Her 1:59.11 shattered the previous NCAA mark and currently is the only collegiate women's time under 2 minutes in the history of the event. Name her and her college.

105. Her muscular physique intimidated most of her competitors before the gun even went off. In 1983—at the debut World Championships in Helsinki—she won both the 400 and 800, the former in what was then a world-record time of 47.99.

A. Anna Quirot of Cuba; B. Marita Koch of East Germany; C. Christine Wachtel of East Germany; D. Jarmila Kratochvilova of Czechoslovakia

106. When he won the 400-and 800-meter races at the Montreal Olympic Games in 1976, it was a rare feat.

A. Alberto Juantorena of Cuba; B. Mike Boit of Kenya; C. Joaquim Cruz of Brazil; D. Julius Sang of Kenya

107. The man who won the Montreal Olympic 800 also broke the world record (1:43.5 to 1:43.7) held by this runner.

A. Marcello Fiasconaro of Italy; B. Roger Moens of Belgium; C. Peter Snell of New Zealand; D. Ralph Doubell of Australia

108. This New York Athletic Club runner achieved the 400-800 double in the 1896 Athens Olympics. A longshot winner in the 400, he then beat fellow American James Lightbody by just one-tenth of a second to win the 800 in 2:01.5. (Hint: His initials are P. P.)

109. This man won an Olympic gold medal in the two-lap race at the 1932 Los Angeles Games with a huge personal best, becoming the first to break 1:50 for 800 meters with 1:49.7—just a few meters ahead of Alexander Wilson of Canada, the second man to ever break 1:50.

A. Thomas Hampson of Great Britain; B. Ben Eastman of the U.S.A.; C. Joaquim Cruz of Brazil; D. Rudolf Harbig of Germany

110. This British runner won back-to-back Olympic gold medals in the 800-meter run.

A. Peter Snell; B. Steve Ovett; C. Sebastian Coe; D. Douglas Lowe

111. Perhaps a surprise entry in the Olympic 800, this man—a champion at a long-distance event in the previous Olympic Games—was forced to settle for bronze in the 1988 Seoul Games. It was his first loss in three years at any distance.

A. Said Aouita of Morocco; B. Sebastian Coe of Great Britain; C. Steve Cram of Great Britain; D. Noureddine Morceli of Algeria

112. The gold in 1988 Olympic 800 went to:

A. Steve Ovett of Great Britain; B. Billy Konchellah of Kenya; C. Joaquim Cruz of Brazil; D. Paul Ereng of Kenya

113. In the history of the NCAA Division I outdoor meet, three men have won three 880-yard/800-meter titles. One was from Indiana and ran in the early 1930s; one from Pittsburgh and ran in the late 1930s; and one competed in the 1990s and ran for Tennessee. Name this select trio.

114. This Fordham grad pushed through the pain barrier ("If I live, I will never run again . . . ," he thought at the time) to outlean Briton Derek Johnson by one-tenth of a second at the Melbourne Olympic Games in 1956. His 1:47.7 was a new Olympic record. Name him.

A. Arnie Sowell; B. Tom Farrell; C. Tom Courtney; D. Mal Whitfield

115. Which country swept all the women's 800-meter medals in the Moscow Olympics—an Olympic first in the women's events?

A. Romania; B. Soviet Union; C. Czechoslovakia; D. East Germany

116. This woman led that sweep with what was then a world record of 1:53.42.

A. Nadezhda Olizarenko of the Soviet Union; B. Sigrun Wodars of East Germany; C. Jarmila Kratochvilova of Czechoslovakia; D. Doina Melinte of Romania

117. This former Pennsylvania high school star went on to win two Olympic medals (silver and bronze, respectively) in the 800 meters in 1984 and 1988.

118. This two-time Olympic 800-meter gold-medal winner says he sometimes sleeps in his old 1948 Olympic team sweats on cold nights.

A. Arthur Wint of Jamaica; B. John Woodruff of the U.S.A.; C. Tom Courtney of the U.S.A.; D. Mal Whitfield of the U.S.A.

119. Name the only U.S. collegiate team—anchored by Mike Stahr's 1:45 leg—to crack 7:10 in the 4 x 800-meter relay with 7:08.96 in 1984.

A. Arizona State; B. Georgetown; C. Penn State; D. Villanova

120. Only the Moscow Olympic boycott stopped this four-time U.S. Olympic Trials champion from competing in four Olympic Games. In 1968 she won the 800 gold at Mexico City and set a new world record of 2:00.9. Name her.

A: Madeline Manning; B. Doris Brown; C. Francie Larrieu-Smith; D. Mary Decker Slaney

121. Although he was turned down by the New York police force because he was thought to have a weak heart, this man trounced the 800-meter field at London in 1908 in a world-record time of 1:52.8. He also won the Olympic 1500 and had two career Olympic golds on the 4 x 400 relay.

A. Merv Albert; B. James Lightbody; C. Melvin Sheppard; D. Ira Davenport

122. In the 1912 Olympic Games, this runner—still a high school student—not only outkicked the defending Olympic champion, but also set a world record of 1:51.9. He later went on to star for the Penn Quakers and also set a world record for 400 meters, blazing 47.4 on cinders.

A. John Paul Jones; B. Paul Pilgrim; C. Cal Coolidge; D. Ted Meredith

123. This 1996 Olympic men's 800-meter champion reportedly did some training in a long tunnel in order to deal with unpleasant weather conditions in his country.

A. Evgeny Arzhanov of the Soviet Union; B. Vebjorn Rodal of Norway; C. Kevin Sullivan of Canada; D. Wilson Kipketer of Denmark

124. SILVER-MEDAL QUESTION. When Paavo Nurmi toured America in 1925, he raced 55 times and won 53 races. He dropped out once. Nurmi's only loss came to this Penn State star—a two-time NCAA champion and a member of the 1924 Olympic gold-medal-winning 4 x 400-meter quartet—at 800 meters, admittedly a very short race for the Finnish star, who excelled at longer races such as 5000 and 10,000-meter events. Who beat Nurmi in this short race?

125. The race was run at this famous New York City sports venue on May 26, 1925:

A. Yankee Stadium; B. Belmont Racetrack; C. The Polo Grounds; D. Madison Square Garden

SPRINTS
ANSWERS

1. D
2. A
3. D
4. C
5. A
6. D
7. D
8. B
9. Cliff Cushman
10. Gail Devers
11. Because the rules of the time stated that a record would be discounted if the runner didn't cleanly clear the hurdles. Tisdale knocked his last hurdle hard and almost stumbled before recovering for the win. Subsequently, Hardin's "clean" (albeit second-place) run was recognized as the new world record.
12. D
13. B
14. C
15. D. Davis won in 1956 and 1960. Moses also won twice (1976 and 1984), but the Moscow boycott was sandwiched in between. Had he been able to compete, Moses would have been a very strong favorite.

16. B
17. O. J. Simpson
18. A
19. A
20. B
21. Herb Washington
22. D
23. A
24. C
25. C
26. A
27. Stella Walsh
28. Tommie Smith won the gold; John Carlos the bronze.
29. D
30. C
31. False. Glenn Ashby Davis, the Olympic hurdler, did play football (in fact, for the NFL Lions and Rams), but—as an Ohio State Buckeye—he should not be confused with the older Glenn Woodward Davis who starred for the Black Knights.
32. B
33. A
34. D
35. D
36. Allen Johnson of the U.S.A.
37. C
38. C
39. Alvin Kraenzlein and John Tewksbury
40. D
41. B
42. D

43. B
44. A
45. C
46. C
47. A
48. B
49. D
50. D
51. D
52. Valery Borzov
53. B
54. Rey Robinson and Eddie Hart
55. B
56. Current WR 100-meter man Asafa Powell of Jamaica; Donovan Bailey of Canada; Armin Hary of West Germany; Harry Jerome of Canada; Lloyd LaBeach of Panama. Ben Johnson of Canada is a debatable answer because of his eventual suspension for performance-enhancing drugs.
57. C
58. D
59. A
60. Ben Johnson
61. A
62. Arthur Wint and V. George Rhoden
63. A
64. C
65. Frank Wykoff, Ralph Metcalfe, and Foy Draper
66. D
67. Marty Glickman and Sam Stoller
68. B

69. A

70. Yordanka Donkova of Bulgaria and Ludmila Engquist of Russia/Sweden

71. True

72. Carl Lewis

73. Leroy Burrell and Dennis Mitchell

74. D

75. C

76. C

77. D

78. B

79. True. As of 2005, she attends USC, but only as a student. She sprints in professional meets.

80. Carl Lewis and Maurice Greene of the U.S.A.; Linford Christie of Great Britain; Donovan Bailey of Canada

81. Marie-Jose Perec

82. A

83. B

84. True

85. B

86. D

87. D. Americans beat him each time, forcing him to settle for three silvers.

88. D

89. C

90. John Baxter Taylor

91. C

92. C

93. D

94. C

95. Peter Elliott, Gary Cook, Steve Cram, Sebastian Coe

96. D

97. When a number of the competitors collapsed at the finish from exhaustion, the International Amateur Athletic Federation (IAAF) banned women from competing in any events longer than 200 meters for the next 32 years.

98. A

99. A

100. C

101. D

102. A

103. D

104. Suzy Favor Hamilton of Wisconsin

105. D

106. A

107. A

108. Paul Pilgrim

109. A

110. D

111. A

112. D

113. Charles Hornbostel of Indiana; John Woodruff of Pitt; Jose Parrilla of Tennessee

114. C

115. B

116. A

117. Kim Gallagher

118. D

119. A
120. A
121. C
122. D
123. B
124. Alan Helffrich
125. A

MILE QUEST

Speaking with the eloquence that no doubt helped elect him to the British Parliament, world-class middle-distance runner Sebastian Coe once said: "Blink and you miss a sprint. The 10,000 meters is lap after lap of waiting. Theatrically, the mile is just the right length—beginning, middle, end, a story unfolding."

Those dramatic properties also make the mile a prime place to mine trivia questions. The great mile matchups—Landy versus Bannister, Ryun and Liquori, Cunningham and Lovelock, Coe and Ovett—take on the aura of heavyweight title fights, and inevitably result in both the grit and glamour of what is arguably track's most celebrated event.

Part of the mile's mystique comes from its rigid requirements to run the race well. If sprinting is the domain of the "world's fastest human" and if the marathon is the accepted standard of Olympic endurance, then the mile taps into both attributes—a blend of endurance and speed is required at the world-class level for any chance at success.

The mile also seems to demand a lot of tactical skills, though the renowned Arthur Lydiard—the famous coach from New Zealand—predicted in the 1970s that "the days of tactics are numbered." Lydiard believed the supermilers of the future would simply be the best-trained, most blessed specimens of racers—all legs and lungs, as the expression goes.

Is it possible—with the men's world record for the mile now

in the low 3:40s—that we will some fine day see some super-runner blast a mile into the 3:30 range? For those of us who grew up running—the 4-minute mile often looming in our dreams like King Arthur and his Round Table knights pursuing the Holy Grail—a sub-3:40 mile might not even *sound* like a mile time; it wasn't too many years ago that 3:39 was a world-class 1500-meter effort.

Back in the 1980s, the British coach Harry Wilson scoffed at our sentimentality concerning the four-minute mile.

"I think it's bloody silly to put flowers on the grave of the 4-minute mile now, isn't it?" Wilson glibly commented. "It turns out it wasn't so much like Everest as it was like the Matterhorn; somebody had to climb it first, but I hear now they've even got a cow up it."

Nevertheless, Sir Roger Bannister's breaking of the 4-minute barrier can almost by itself generate a chapter of trivia. I didn't go quite that far, but certainly you're well "tuned in" to this trivia game if you can identify the American runner who competed in that now historic mile race at Oxford's Iffley Road track on May 6, 1954. (This question would be easy money for my former *Runner's World* colleague Dave Kuehls, who once interviewed that particular American runner in conjunction with the 50th anniversary of Bannister's grand accomplishment.)

Similarly, it would be impossible to tap into the trivia of the mile without dozens of questions involving Jim Ryun—and some of those include one of America's top milers on the scene today, Alan Webb.

The mile, too, seems to be one of those events that even the average sports fan has a vague idea about. For example, if you tell the average nontrack sports fan that you ran 4 minutes, 32 seconds for the mile, he might respond with a look of respect and recognition. Tell the same nontrack sports fan you clocked 29:58 for 10,000 meters, and my bet is he'll ask you: "Is that good?" or "How far is that exactly?"

And the answer to how far the 10,000-meter event actually is depends on whether the lap counter is paying full attention to his assigned duties. But you rarely see even the most clueless track official mess up the laps in the mile. Four laps just has a certain symmetry to it—simultaneously simplistic and majestic.

1. When the British professional Walter George ran 4:12-3/4 for the mile in London in August 1886, many observers of that era adamantly believed it was a mark that would never be broken. Just how long *did* it take until someone ran (ever-so-slightly) faster?

A. 11 months; B. almost a decade; C. about 29 years; D. nearly 50 years

2. Because Walter George was a professional, one of the first amateur mile records to be listed for the mile was credited to this American—who had the same name as a famous naval hero. He ran 4:14.4 in 1913.

A. John Paul Jones; B. William Halsey; C. Oliver Perry; D. David Farragut

3. Name the U.S. Olympian who finally bettered George's time in Cambridge, Massachusetts.

A. Abel Kivat; B. James Lightbody; C. Joie Ray; D. Norman Taber

4. This man still has the fastest mile of all time with 3:43.13 (as of September 2005)

A. Said Aouita of Morocco; B. Noureddine Moceli of Algeria; C. Sebastian Coe of Great Britain; D. Hicham El Guerrouj of Morocco

5. On July 7, 1982, in Oslo, Norway, one of the most prolific world-class milers in history popped a 3:47.69 mile—the second fastest in history at the time (to Seb Coe's world record 3:47.33). His winning performance that night is still the American record.

A. Jim Spivey; B. Tom Byers; C. Steve Scott; D. Jim Ryun

6. His time of 3:29.77 for 1500 meters—clocked in 1985—is still the American record and puts him tied with Briton Sebastian Coe on the all-time world list.

A. Jim Spivey; B. Sydney Maree; C. Steve Scott; D. Steve Holman

7. Name the pair of Swedes who took turns setting the world record for the mile six times in about three years time between the summers of 1942 and 1945.

8. This Briton, a world-record holder, was the first man to run 4:00.0 for a mile.

A. Sydney Wooderson; B. Roger Bannister; C. Gordon Pirie; D. Derek Ibbotson

9. On May 6, 1954, what watershed event occurred in Oxford, England, at the Iffley Road track?

A. Roger Bannister ran 3:59-flat to record history's first sub-four minute mile; B. Bannister clocked 3:59.4; C. Bannister ran 3:58.8; D. Bannister ran 3:59.9

10. In the days prior to the event, Bannister did what in an attempt to relax before taking on what was then regarded as "the Everest" of middle-distance running?

A. went hiking in Scotland; B. relaxed on the beach in Majorca, Spain; C. played Prince Hamlet in a local Shakespeare production; D. groomed the cinder track at Iffley Road to calm his nerves

11. How many men lined up to race on that historic day?

A. 3; B. 9; C. 6; D. 12

12. The man who finished *last* in the race was an American student at Oxford, with approximate lifetime bests of 1:56 for the half mile and 4:15 for the mile. His name was:

A. Ronald McDonald; B. George Best; C. Eric Clapton; D. George Dole

13. Bannister seriously contemplated not racing that day because:

A. It was somewhat windy; B. Steady rain from the previous night had left the inside lane of the cinder track muddy; C. He had a bad cold; D. He had worked a 12-hour shift at the hospital where he was a medical student; E. All of the above

14. Bannister's primary pacemakers that day were:

A. John Landy and Wes Santee; B. Chris Brasher and Chris Chataway; C. Percy Cerutty and Herb Elliott; D. David Moorcroft and Gordon Pirie

15. Approximately how many people attended what is now regarded as one of track's most historic performances?

A. 12; B. 120; C. 1,200; D. 12,000

16. What popular American television game show tried to get Roger Bannister to appear shortly after his grand achievement?

A. *What's My Line?* B. *Hollywood Squares;* C. *I've Got a Secret;* D. *Wheel of Fortune*

17. FRENCH BENEFIT. In the aftermath of his glittering accomplishment, Bannister said this in French: *Après moi, le deluge.* This roughly translates to:

18. Bannister's new world record lasted just 46 days, when Australian John Landy blasted 3:58 for the mile. Landy ran the race at:

A. Olympic Park, Melbourne, Australia; B. Bislett Stadium, Oslo, Norway; C. London's White City Stadium; D. the city stadium in Torku, Finland

19. If Bannister's record was relatively short lived, consider this: On August 26, 1981, Great Britain's Steve Ovett clocked a new world record of 3:48.40 for the mile. Fellow Brit and archrival Sebastian Coe broke it

A. one week later; B. 2 days later; C. 11 days later; D. 3 hours later

20. At the 1954 Empire Games staged in Vancouver, British Columbia, what was the similarity between Roger Bannister and John Landy's qualifying heats in the mile?

A. Both came in third, content to qualify and save their energy for the final; B. Both had shoelaces come untied, but still managed to qualify; C. Both suffered spike wounds, but were not seriously injured; D. Both runners clocked 4:01 and change, just cruising

21. The buildup and publicity for the Bannister-Landy race was so huge that the event was billed as:

A. The Greatest Race on Earth; B. The Battle of the British Empire; C. The Mile of the Century; D. The Dream Mile

22. This magazine sent journalists to cover the race for its premiere issue:

A. *Track & Field News;* B. *Life;* C. *Sports Illustrated;* D. *Distance Running News*

23. Although this detail has most likely been overblown, some "experts" believe this action may have cost John Landy the race.

A. He swung slightly wide coming off the last turn, allowing

Bannister to slip by on the inside; B. He broke the wind for Bannister for more than three-quarters of the race; C. He glanced back over his inside shoulder—just as Bannister made his charge for the lead; D. He set too slow a pace over the first lap

24. Lost in the excitement of the Bannister-Landy duel upfront, this man finished third in the Empire Games mile, but didn't break 4-minutes.

A. Wes Santee of the U.S.A.; B. William Baillie of New Zealand; C. Rich Ferguson of Canada; D. Murray Halberg of New Zealand

25. In addition to the crowd of 35,000-plus in Empire Stadium, the worldwide television/radio audience for the race was estimated at:

A: 12 million; B. 28 million; C. 58 million; D. 100 million

26. This Princeton man clocked a 4:08 mile in 1933—a Tiger record that stood for 35 years. (Hint: He also held the WR for 1500 meters at 3:47.8 in the 1930s.)

A. Archie San Romani; B. Bill Bonthron; C. John F. Cregan; D. Ian Douglas Mackenzie

27. Playing 18 holes of golf and wolfing down a quart of vanilla ice cream the morning before his evening mile race probably didn't

help the above Tiger star when he faced this man in a 1934 mile matchup at Princeton. The visitor won in a world record of 4:06.8.

A. Louis Zamperini of Southern Cal; B. Gene Venske of Penn; C. Glenn Cunningham of Kansas; D. Jack Lovelock of New Zealand

28. This great miler, a world-record holder and an Olympic medal winner, suffered severe burns on his legs (caused by an exploding stove) when he was just 13 years old. It was thought by some that he would never walk again. He began running to make his legs strong.

A. Abel Kiviat; B. James Lightbody; C. Glenn Cunningham; D. Jack Lovelock

29. In 1938 this man was invited to Dartmouth University in New Hampshire to attempt a new indoor world record in the mile. Paced by a relay of Dartmouth runners on the banked track, he clocked 4:04.4, well under the existing mile records both indoors and out. But the record was disallowed because the meet had not been sanctioned. Who ran the 4:04?

A. Jack Lovelock of New Zealand; B. Bill Bonthron of Princeton; C. Glenn Cunningham of Kansas; D. Gunder Hägg of Sweden

30. Roger Bannister clocked his historic sub-4 mile on May 6, 1954. The first American (the 12th man in the world to do it)

achieved this feat in what year, and in what time?

A. 1955 in a time of 3:55.9; B. 1956 in a time of 3:56.6; C. 1957 in a time of 3:58.7; D. 1964 in a time of 3:58.2

31. And who *was* the first American runner to break the 4-minute mile?

A. Wes Santee of Kansas; B. Jim Beatty of North Carolina; C. Jim Grelle of Oregon; D. Don Bowden of UC-Berkeley

32. In a race chasing Jim Ryun and Kip Keino in 1966, this man became the first Canadian to break 4 minutes in the mile with a 3:59.1. A year later he popped a 3:57.7 on Canadian soil.

A. Rich Ferguson; B. Ben Johnson; C. Bill Crothers; D. David Bailey

33. When he first broke 4 minutes for the mile at the Compton Invitational Mile in June 1964, high school junior Jim Ryun was racing against seven experienced veteran milers. Dyrol Burleson of Oregon won the race in 3:57.4. What place did Ryun finish?

A. second, about 4 yards behind; B. second in a photo finish; C. fifth; D. last

34. He's the only one to break the 4-minute mile in a high-school-runners-only race.

A. Alan Webb; B. Jim Ryun; C. Marty Liquori; D. Tim Danielson

35. Jim Ryun suffered a rare loss to another high school runner in an indoor mile on San Francisco's Cow Palace board track in 1963. Ryun fell at the start, hurting his chances. The high school runner who won was:

A. Gerry Lindgren; B. Rick Riley; C. Marty Liquori; D. Tim Danielson

36. A national-class miler at Villanova in the 1950s, this man went on to coach Marty Liquori at Essex Catholic in New Jersey—and allegedly suggested that Marty quit playing his rock-and-roll guitar.

A. Jim "Jumbo" Elliott; B. Jack Pyrah; C. Noel Carroll; D. Fred Dwyer

37. A former football player and wrestler, he was the second high school runner to break 4 minutes when he clocked 3:59.4 on the new all-weather track at Balboa Stadium in San Diego. He had less than two years of running experience when he accomplished this feat!

A. Rick Riley; B. Gerry Lindgren; C. Marty Liquori; D. Tim Danielson

38. Although he certainly isn't remembered as a miler, his 4:01.5 (when compared with 1600-meter equivalents) is still the high school record in Washington State.

A. Rick Riley; B. Gerry Lindgren; C. Len Long; D. Don Kardong

39. He was the first high school runner to break 4:10 for the mile, and later went on to run for the University of Oregon.

A. Archie San Romani Jr.; B. Dyrol Burleson; C. Jim Grelle; D. Bill Dellinger

40. Who coached the above runner in high school?

A. Bob Timmons; B. Bill Bowerman; C. Wes Santee; D. Bill Hayward

41. Who was the first Kansas runner to break the 4-minute mile?

A. Archie San Romani Jr.; B. Jim Ryun; C. Glenn Cunningham; D. Bill Dotson; E. Wes Santee; F. Jerome Howe

42. In 1962 who was the first man to break four-minutes for the mile on an indoor track?

A. Herb Elliott of Australia; B. Jim Beatty of the U.S.A.; C. Michel Jazy of France; D. Tom O'Hara of the U.S.A.

43. In what city did this feat take place?

A. Los Angeles; B. Boston; C. San Francisco; D. New York City

44. A high school runner, Jim Ryun made his first U.S. Olympic team when he nipped this veteran American miler (and former 1959 NCAA champ from Oregon) in a sprint for the last spot on the 1964 U.S. Olympic 1500-meter team. (Hint: Ryun also broke this man's American record in the mile when he clocked a 3:55.3 mile in 1965 and once held him off by inches to set a U.S. 2-mile record.)

A. Jim Grelle; B. Jim Beatty; C. Tom O'Hara; D. Dyrol Burleson

45. In 1965, still in high school, Ryun upset this Olympic champion in a mile race that also helped the Kansas boy snare the U.S. mile record with a 3:55.3.

A. Billy Mills, U.S.A.; B. Bob Schul, U.S.A.; C. Peter Snell of New Zealand; D. Ron Delaney of Ireland

46. This two-time NCAA mile champion from USC was captured

by the Japanese and held in a POW camp during World War II.

A. Eric Liddell; B. Butch Reynolds; C. Colin Smith; D. Louis Zamperini

47. A winner of two silver medals (1500 and 800) in Montreal, this Belgian star died in a car crash just months after his outstanding Olympic races. A major track meet in Brussels is named in his honor.

A. Gaston Roelants; B. Emiel Puttemans; C. Roger Moens; D. Ivo van Damme

48. On February 13, 1964, at Madison Square Garden, Tom O'Hara blasted a 55-second last quarter to smash Jim Beatty's indoor world record for the mile, clocking 3:56.6. Who was the guest starter for that race?

A. Roger Bannister; B. Jim Beatty; C. Herb Elliott; D. John Landy

49. In 1983, at the Meadowlands in New Jersey, he became the first man to break 3:50 for the mile indoors.

A. Ray Flynn of Ireland; B. John Walker of New Zealand; C. Eamonn Coghlan of Ireland; D. Marcus O'Sullivan of Ireland

50. These two runners from the 1950s were so close that race officials often had to hold lengthy meetings to determine a winner and the *New York Times* dubbed them "The Inseparables." One was a three-time NCAA mile/1500 champ from Wisconsin, the other a former NCAA cross-country champ from Indiana, an FBI man, and, in the 1960s, the coach of marathoner Buddy Edelen.

51. Nicknamed "Mr. Unpredictable" because of his erratic racing performances, this Finn held off Kip Keino to clinch the 1500-meter gold medal at the Munich Games in 1972.

A. Pekka Vasala; B. Kaarlo Maaninka; C. Juha Vaatainen; D. Lasse Viren

52. His 3:52.87 broke Noureddine Morceli's Madison Square Garden record and Eamonn Coghlan's long-standing Millrose Games mark in February 2005.

A. Alan Webb; B. Bernard Lagat; C. Hicham El Guerrouj; D. Timothy Kiptanui

53. U.S. champ Jim Ryun never made it to the final because he fell in a trial heat. The African runner who fell with him was:

A. Kip Keino of Kenya; B. Billy Fordjour of Ghana; C. Mike Boit of Kenya; D. Filbert Bayi of Tanzania

54. Which of these things happened at Jim Ryun's mile race at UC-Berkeley in 1967?

A. All his warm-up gear was stolen from the athletes' tent while he was giving postrace interviews; B. He blew off his future wife, Anne, when she approached him for a postrace autograph; C. He set a world record in the mile with 3:51.3; D. All of the above

55. Jim Ryun set several world records in his career, but this was the only one he set in Kansas.

A. the world indoor 880 record; B. the 1500-meter record; C. the 880-yard outdoor record; D. his first world record in the mile

56. Some "experts" of the sport credit this man's kamikaze pace-setting (56.0 opening 400)—all the more taxing in the high altitude—for setting up Kip Keino's gold-medal win over Jim Ryun in the 1968 Olympic 1500. (Hint: He scored an Olympic silver in the steeplechase at Munich in 1972.)

A. Amos Biwott of Kenya; B. Ben Jipcho of Kenya; C. Mike Boit of Kenya; D. Yobes Ondieki of Kenya

57. Early in his career, one of Kip Keino's habits during a race was to do this:

A: Run in lane two for the entire race; B. Pump his right fist in the air just before going into his final kick; C. Talk to his opponents in Swahili; D. Toss a hat he wore onto the infield just before sprinting away from the pack

58. Who said: "I didn't have Olympic luck. I had other luck and silver medals. Remember, to be second behind Herb Elliott is like being an Olympic champion."

A. John Landy of Australia; B. Michel Jazy of France; C. Merv Lincoln of Austalia; D. Derek Ibbotson of Great Britain

59. Australia's John Landy was nicknamed "Gentleman John"—in part because he stopped to help this then-19-year-old runner (who was destined to race better at longer distances) when the teen fell in a mile race. (Landy, despite his stop, rallied to chase down the leaders and win this 1956 race.)

A. Albie Thomas; B. Herb Elliott; C. Ron Clarke; D. Merv Lincoln

60. Although he retired quite early by today's standards, 1960 1500-meter Olympic champ Herb Elliott never lost a 1500 or mile race in his career. Approximately how many wins in that event did Elliott post?

A. 22; B. 33; C. 39; D. 44

61. Despite Elliott's stellar record, one of his archrivals *did* once tie his time (although race officials picked Elliott—by inches—as the winner): Both men clocked in 3:59.6 on a grass track in Perth in 1958. Who was this fellow Australian, who spent most of his career in Elliott's shadow?

A. Albie Thomas; B. Brian Lenton; C. Ron Clarke; D. Merv Lincoln

62. A mile in Dublin in 1958—despite a half-hour delay to clear spectators from the outer lanes prior to the event and a dog dashing out on the track during the third lap—resulted in a nearly 3-second slash from Derek Ibbotson's world record of 1957. Who clocked this 3:54.5 world record?

A. Herb Elliott of Australia; B. Peter Snell of New Zealand; C. Michel Jazy of France; D. Ronnie Delaney of Ireland

63. The Marty Liquori-Jim Ryun rivalry was huge in the early 1970s. In a classic race, Liquori's long kick held off Ryun's stretch-drive challenge, winning in 3:54.6. In what stadium and in what city was this matchup staged?

A. Memorial Stadium, Lawrence, Kansas; B. Hayward Field, Eugene, Oregon; C. Palmer Stadium, Princeton, New Jersey; D. Franklin Field, Philadelphia, Pennsylvania

64. Part of the Martin Luther King Jr. Games, what was this great mile event called?

A. The Miracle Mile; B. The King of the Mile; C. The Mile of the Century; D. The Dream Mile

65. With 13 first-place finishes in the men's NCAA Division I outdoor 1500/mile event, this school has the most individual titles in this middle-distance glamour event that's been contested since 1921.

A. Arkansas; B. Oregon; C. Kansas; D. Villanova

66. With a 3:57.1 clocking, his mile from the 1970s still stands as the NCAA D-I outdoor best, although there have been 1500 equivalents since then that, if converted, are faster.

A. Jim Ryun of Kansas; B. Dyrol Burleson of Oregon; C. Marty Liquori of Villanova; D. Dave Wottle of Bowling Green

67. Two of Alan's Webb's greatest miles—his 3:53.46 that snapped Jim Ryun's 36-year-old high school mark and recently a 3:50.85, the fastest mile run by an American on U.S. soil—both happened on this track.

A. Franklin Field, Philadelphia; B. Memorial Stadium, Lawrence, Kansas; C. The Los Angeles Coliseum; D. Hayward Field, Eugene, Oregon

68. "I lost my first race at school and I was so jealous when the winner received a puppet that I said to myself: 'I will carry on until I win a puppet.'" The runner who said that currently holds the world record in the women's mile (4:12.56) and won Olympic gold medals in the 800- and 1500-meter runs. Who is she?

A. Paula Ivan of Romania; B. Tatyana Kazankina of the Soviet Union; C. Sletvana Masterkova of Russia; D. Gabriella Dorio of Italy

69. Twice this American held the world record in the women's mile.

A. Suzy Favor Hamilton; B. Marla Runyan; C. Francie Larrue Smith; D. Mary Decker Slaney

70. No woman has won three NCAA Division I titles in the 1500 meters. But one woman *has* won four! She also holds the collegiate record (4:08.26) for the outdoor 1500 and the indoor NCAA D-I mile (4:30.63) through 2005. Name her.

A. Amy Rudolph, Providence; B. Vicki Huber, Villanova; C. Suzy Favor Hamilton, Wisconsin; D. Mary Decker Slaney, Colorado

71. SILVER-MEDAL QUESTION Name the three middle distance greats who have run more than 100 sub-4-minute miles.

72. He was so good at the indoor mile that he was called "The Chairman of the Boards," and John Walker (all in good fun!) allegedly once said: "When you hear the crowd noise, it means that little bastard has made his move."

A. Said Aouita of Morocco; B. Marcus O'Sullivan of Ireland.; C. Eamonn Coghlan of Ireland; D. Rod Dixon of New Zealand

73. At age 41, at a meet removed from the spotlight indoors at Harvard, he became the first master to break 4-minutes for the mile.

A. John Walker of New Zealand; B. Steve Scott of the U.S.A.; C. Eamonn Coghlan of Ireland; D. Rod Dixon of New Zealand

74. Who was the first African runner to set the world record for the mile?

A. Said Aouita of Morocco; B. Filbert Bayi of Tanzania; C. Kip Keino of Kenya; D. Noureddine Morceli of Algeria

75. This great British middle-distance runner reportedly contemplated running for West Germany (his mother's birthplace) because of the intense competition to make the UK team.

A. David Moorcroft; B. Brendan Foster; C. Steve Cram; D. Steve Ovett

76. After he won the Olympic 1500 in 1984, he immediately made a defiant gesture at British sportswriters sitting in the stands and shouted: "Who says I'm through?"

A. Steve Ovett; B. Sebastian Coe; C. Steve Cram; D. Peter Elliott

77. In the mid-1980s this former Villanova runner was one of the few runners to briefly intrude on British dominance in the 1500, setting a World (and U.S.) record in West Germany with 3:31.24.

A. Sydney Maree; B. Marcus O'Sullivan; C. Eamonn Coghlan; D. Don Paige

78. The runner who finished second in the 1984 Olympic 1500 went on to become the first man in history to break 3:30 for 1500 meters.

A. Said Aouita of Morocco; B. Steve Ovett of Great Britain; C. Steve Cram of Great Britain; D. Peter Rono of Kenya

79. This French middle distance star (who once held the world record in the mile and 1500 meters, and snagged an Olympic silver medal in the latter event) was bothered by pre-race nerves to such a degree that he often needed a massage right before the event to relax.

A. Michel Jazy; B. Jules Ladoumegue; C. Alain Mimoun; D. Guy Drut

80. John Walker of New Zealand was the first man to crack 3:50 for the mile, clocking 3:49.4 in Goteborg, Sweden, in 1975. In addition to about $300 in expense money, what did race promoters reportedly provide for Walker as a reward for his landmark achievement?

A. A silver stopwatch, with "3:49.4" engraved on the back; B. a case of beer; C. a photo op with blond Swedish models on each arm, à la the Tour de France awards ceremony; D. a dinner with the King of Sweden in Stockholm

81. John Walker, running 3:32.5, was under Jim Ryun's 6½-year-old world 1500-meter record of 3:33.1 at the Commonwealth Games, staged in Christchurch, New Zealand, in 1974. The only problem is, this guy beat John to the finish, clocking 3:32.2!

A. Filbert Bayi of Tanzania; B. Mike Boit of Kenya; C. Ben Jipcho of Kenya; D. Rod Dixon of New Zealand

82. The Commonwealth Games 1500 was so fast that this man finished fifth, but broke Herb Elliott's long-standing Australian national record with 3:34.2.

A. Steve Moneghetti; B. Brian Lenton; C. Graham Crouch; D. Dick Quax

83. One of Roger Bannister's early career coups came in the U.S.A. in 1951 when he won:

A. the Wanamaker Mile at the Millrose Games in Madison Square Garden; B. the Ben Franklin Mile at the Penn Relays in Philadelphia; C. the Glenn Cunningham Mile at the Kansas Relays; D. the feature mile race at the Drake Relays in Iowa

84. Despite his successes later in his career, Roger Bannister failed to medal in the 1952 Helsinki Olympic Games. He attributed his fourth place finish at the time to his inability to:

A. cope with big-meet pressure; B. deliver his powerful kick; C. deal with the aggressive in-pack jostling and elbowing from the veteran runners; D. recover from racing several energy-sapping trial heats

85. This Olympian was the only New Zealander to simultaneously hold the world records in both the 1500 meters and the mile.

A. John Walker; B. Peter Snell; C. Jack Lovelock; D. Rod Dixon

86. When Peter Snell set the world record in the mile of 3:54.4 in New Zealand in 1962, the appreciative crowd of 16,000 responded by:

A. singing "For He's a Jolly Good Fellow"; B. tossing a less-than-enthused Snell in the steeplechase water jump; C. carrying him around the track on their shoulders; D. giving him a standing ovation that lasted 4 minutes

87. In 1981 Briton Steve Ovett and other world-class milers raced a 1500 meters at Bislett Stadium, Oslo, Norway. But a "rabbit" hired to take the field through a fast 1200 ended up stealing the race. Who was this former Ohio State runner?

A. Don Paige; B. Tom Byers; C. Rick Wohlhuter, D. Paul Pilkington

88. This miler from North Carolina had a relatively brief career at the top, but in 1974 he was hotter than Las Vegas in July—including a world-record 3:55.0 in San Diego to shatter the indoor mile mark that was co-held by Tom O'Hara and Jim Ryun.

A. Abel Kivat; B. Jim Beatty; C. Tony Waldrop; D. Howell Michaels

89. He ran the fastest indoor mile (3:59.86) by a high school runner ever.

A. Alan Webb; B. Jim Ryun; C. Marty Liquori; D. Steve Prefontaine

90. A very slow tactical race helped set up this man's furious sprint finish to win the Olympic 1500-meter gold at Barcelona in 1992—much to the delight of the fans. He managed a silver in Atlanta four years later.

A. Said Aouita of Morocco; B. Peter Rono of Kenya; C. Noureddine Morceli of Algeria; D. Fermin Cacho of Spain

91. This Olympic champ from New Zealand is honored by a statue and an oak tree at the Timaru Boys' High School—where he once attended classes.

A. Jack Lovelock; B. Peter Snell; C. Murray Halberg; D. John Walker

92. After his retirement, Roger Bannister often rewarded other runners who broke the 4-minute mile barrier with this:

A. an autographed copy of his book *The Four Minute Mile;* B. a free beer at his favorite Oxford pub; C. a black silk tie with monogrammed letters—a silver "4" and a pair of gold Ms within a laurel wreath; D. an autographed photograph from the original sub-4 race

93. Which of these things *didn't* happen to miler Wes Santee, "the Kansas Flyer"?

A. He was suspended from amateur competition for alleged expense violations; B. He eventually broke 4 minutes for the mile; C. Although he was better at track, he also was an NCAA champ in cross-country; D. He won an Olympic bronze medal in the 1500 at Helsinki in 1952

94. While Wes Santee and Fred Dwyer were bumping each other around in the 1955 Wanamaker Mile, this Scandinavian runner was busy winning the Madison Square Garden race in what was then a world record (4:03.6) for the indoor mile.

A. Gundar Hägg of Sweden; B. Eric Ny of Sweden; C. Gunnar Nielsen of Denmark; D. Lennart Strand of Sweden

95. Three women have won both the 1500 and 800 in the Olympic Games. Name the British woman who achieved this feat in Athens.

A. Ann Packer; B. Christina Boxer; C. Wendy Sly; D. Kelly Holmes

96. Only one British man in the history of the Olympic Games has won both the 800 and 1500. He was:

A. Albert Hill; B. Steve Ovett; C. Sebastian Coe; D. Peter Snell

97. In a span of just 41 days, this British runner set world records in the 800, mile, and 1500 meters.

A. Sydney Wooderson; B. Roger Bannister; C. Sebastian Coe; D. Steve Ovett

98. This American 800-1500 runner held the world record in the seldom run 1000-meter event, until Sebastian Coe broke it by half a second in 1980. Who was he?

A. Jim Ryun; B. Steve Scott; C. Marty Liquori; D. Rick Wohlhuter

99. Name three former world record holders in the men's mile who later held high political office.

100. He might have won an Olympic 1500 medal at the Atlanta Olympic Games, but he tripped on the lead runner coming into the bell lap.

A. Noureddine Morceli of Algeria; B. Abdi Bile of Somalia; C. Steve Cram of Great Britain; D. Hicham El Guerrouj of Morocco

101. This U.S. hopeful for the 1992 Barcelona Games had a 3:49 mile to his credit when he tripped in a crowded 14-man final field in the U.S. Olympic Trials. Name this former NCAA champion.

A. Joe Falcon; B. Steve Holman; C. Jim Spivey; D. Steve Scott

102. Chasing teammate Tony Waldrop at a race in Raleigh, this man became the first African American to crack the 4-minute mile with a 3:59.3 in 1973.

A. Reggie McAfee; B. Byron Dyce; C. Ted Corbitt; D. Denis Fikes

MILE QUEST
ANSWERS

1. C
2. A
3. D
4. D
5. C
6. B
7. Arne Andersson and Gundar Hägg of Sweden
8. D
9. B
10. A
11. C
12. D
13. A
14. B
15. C
16. C
17. "After me, the flood."
18. D
19. B
20. A
21. C

22. C
23. C
24. C
25. D
26. B
27. C
28. C
29. C
30. C
31. D
32. D
33. D
34. B
35. A
36. D
37. D
38. B
39. A
40. A
41. D. Bill Dotson ran 3:59-flat for the mile on June 23, 1962—only the seventh American to do it. Dotson ran for KU. San Romani Jr. (who ran for Oregon in college, but ran high school track in Kansas) was second to do it; Ryun third. Cunningham and Santee never did it. Jerome Howe did do it, but he ran for rival Kansas State.
42. B
43. A
44. A
45. C
46. D

47. D
48. B
49. C
50. Don Gehrmann and Fred Wilt
51. A
52. B
53. B
54. D
55. A
56. B
57. D
58. B
59. C
60. D
61. D
62. A
63. D
64. D
65. D
66. D
67. D
68. C
69. D
70. C
71. John Walker of New Zealand; Steve Scott of the U.S.A.; and Marcus O'Sullivan of Ireland
72. C
73. C
74. B
75. C

76. B

77. A

78. C

79. B

80. B

81. A

82. C

83. B

84. D

85. C

86. A

87. B

88. C

89. A

90. D

91. A

92. C

93. B and D didn't happen.

94. C

95. D

96. A

97. C

98. D

99. Sebastian Coe of Great Britain, John Landy of Australia, Jim Ryun of the U.S.A.

100. D

101. A

102. A

DISTANCE ACES

(Steeplechase, 5000 meters, 10,000 meters,
2 Miles, 3000 meters, etc.)

American running star Billy Mills tells a story about how his daughter asked to take his Olympic gold medal to school one day for show-and-tell. Curious to see what his daughter would say to the class about his achievement, Mills tagged along and sat in the back of the classroom.

His daughter got up before the class, showed them the Olympic gold medal, and then said something like: "This is an Olympic gold medal . . . just like the one Peggy Fleming won for ice skating."

Never mind that more than a few Olympic experts list Mills's victory as one of the most dramatic in the history of the Games; his daughter had her own vision of what an Olympic great was, and it involved wearing figure skates and twisting midair jumps—not track spikes and a furious sprint to the finish in an outside lane.

You do have to be a real distance-running fan (which I am) to appreciate the longer track races, such as the 5000- and 10,000-meter runs. A venue like Franklin Field in Philadelphia, under the lights, or the famous Mt. SAC races inevitably draw the serious distance racers and the hard-core fans of our sport.

Admittedly, though, watching 25-lap races is not everybody's idea of an exciting time. Neil Morgan, a sprint coach whom I've known for many years, is likely to refer to a 5000-meter race on the track as "a two-hotdog event." Similarly, the 10,000 meters would be at least a "three-hotdog event." For Neil, a marathon, no doubt, would be justification to consume an entire side of beef.

American steeplechaser Mike Manley once termed his event "plastic cross-country." With its ever-tricky water jump pit, the steeple frequently fires up a lot of drama—and there's always the potential for a comedy of errors to unfold. At smaller meets, in which the fans are allowed to move around at will, watch how many people gravitate over toward the water jump pit once the steeplechase gets started. It's almost like kids at the local pool waiting for someone to suffer a resounding bellyflop off the high dive, or something.

No wonder the Oregon coach Bill Bowerman once made Kenny Moore take gymnastics. "If I plan to enter this particular young man in the steeplechase, I owe it to his parents to make sure he knows how to fall without killing himself. I made him take swimming last year."

All this predictably results in some interesting trivia concerning the event. In some instances we've got miscounted laps, near disqualifications, and fallen runners who must be hurdled (in addition to the regular obstacles!)—and that's just talking about the Olympic Games.

Women have only been running the 3000-meter steeplechase in competition for a few years now. Amazingly, they are already poised to shatter the 9-minute mark in the event.

I was tempted to place a question in the body of this chapter that asks: "What animal is sometimes placed in water jump pits during steeplechase races?" No, it's not crocodiles or piranhas, although that would admittedly add a whole different intensity level to the event. (Answer: goldfish or carp.)

But that question is sort of one of those that creates even more questions. For example, I wonder why PETA (People for the Ethical Treatment of Animals) hasn't cracked down on that particularly barbaric practice? But it also brings up this question as well: What sins does one commit in a past life in order to be reincarnated as a goldfish sentenced to a stint in a steeplechase pit?

1. In 1978 this man set four world records (3000, steeplechase, 5000 and 10,000 meters) in 80 days.

A. Henry Rono of Kenya; B. Dick Quax of New Zealand; C. Ron Clarke of Australia; D. Moses Tanui of Kenya

2. In 1942 this runner went on a ferocious tear—setting or re-setting 10 world records in 12 weeks—the last of which made him the first man to ever break 14 minutes for 5000 meters (13:58.2). Name him and his country.

3. In the midst of the Cold War, this high school runner soundly beat highly ranked Russian runners in U.S.A.-Soviet dual meet in the 10,000-meter run. The Los Angeles Coliseum crowd of 50,000—delirious with joy—included U.S. Attorney General Bobby Kennedy, who reportedly was moved to tears by the heroic performance.

A. Louis Zamperini; B. Billy Mills; C. Gerry Lindgren; D. Steve Prefontaine

4. This man set the world record for 10,000 meters five times during his career.

A. Paavo Nurmi of Finland; B. Kenenisa Bekele of Ethiopia; C. Emil Zatopek of Czechoslovakia; D. Ville Ritola of Finland

5. Hannes Kolehmainen of Finland, a strong favorite, won the 1912 Stockholm Olympic 10,000-meter run (31:20). But this U.S. team member—a Hopi tribe member from Arizona—held off Albin Stenroos to land a silver medal and break up Finland's 1-2 punch. It would be 52 years before an American would win a medal in that event again. Name him.

6. He was the only non-Finn to win the Olympic 10,000-meter gold, from 1912 through 1936, and he set an Olympic record in the process. Just 33 years old, he was shot in the Palmiry Forest in 1940 during the Nazi occupation of his country.

A. Juri Lossmann of Estonia; B. Janusz Kusocinski of Poland; C. Joseph Guillemot of France; D. Rudolf Hansen of Denmark

7. **BRONZE-MEDAL QUESTION.** The world-record holder for 10,000 meters heading into the 1984 Los Angeles Games, this

European runner proved victorious in his trial heat, but—reportedly plagued by nerves—ducked out halfway through the final and ran out the stadium tunnel. Name him.

8. This famous and popular champion gave one of his Olympic gold medals to another great runner (who never won an Olympic gold), along with a note that read: "Not out of friendship, but because you deserve it." The surprised recipient did have an Olympic bronze and had set numerous world records. Name both men.

9. What great runner is famous for the Olympic feat known as "the double-double"?

A. Paavo Nurmi of Finland; B. Peter Snell of New Zealand; C. Lasse Viren of Finland; D. Emil Zatopek of Czechoslovakia

10. His 10,000-meter victory in the 1964 Tokyo Olympic Games is generally considered to be one of the biggest upsets ever seen in distance running—though the man who performed the feat might disagree.

A. Alberto Cova of Italy; B. Billy Mills of the U.S.A.; C. Bob Schul of the U.S.A.; D. Mohammed Gammoudi of Tunisia

11. This Soviet star—an expert at abruptly changing paces during

races—won double gold at the Melbourne Olympics in 1956, though he later died of a heart attack at just age 48.

A. Yevgeny Arzhanov; B. Pyotr Bolotnikov; C. Vladimir Kuts; D. Leonid Moseyev

12. The 10,000-meter men's mark took a huge tumble—nearly 36 seconds—when Australia's Ron Clarke cranked out 27:39 in Oslo, Norway, in 1965. Who held the previous mark?

A. Vladimir Kuts of the Soviet Union; B. Pyotr Bolotnikov of the Soviet Union; C. Ron Clarke of Australia; D. Sandor Iharos of Hungary

13. Little known outside Northern Europe, steeplechaser Claus Boersen helped Clarke achieve his world record in Oslo (along with a more experienced long-distance runner Jim Hogan). How did Boersen assist Clarke?

A. By agreeing to jump into an event—the 10,000—he rarely ran; international rules required at least three men in a race for a WR to count; B. By pacing Clarke for the first 5000 meters; C. cheering and urging Clarke on during the gun lap, after Boersen had been lapped; D. the Danish runner was able to interpret Norwegian— none of the race officials spoke English

14. She set six world records in 1982, including at 5000 and 10,000 meters.

A. Ingrid Kristiansen of Norway; B. Olga Bondarenko of the Soviet Union; C. Zola Budd of South Africa; D. Mary Decker Slaney of the U.S.A.

15. A serious rugby injury as a teen left this runner with a less-than mobile left arm, but it didn't stop this man from running fast. Attacking with three laps to go, he hung on to win the 5000-meter run at the 1960 Rome Olympic Games.

A. Harald Norpoth of West Germany; B. Murray Halberg of New Zealand; C. Mohammed Gammoudi of Tunisia; D. Gordon Pirie of Great Britain

16. Why did the fans at the 1992 Barcelona Olympic Games whistle (the European equivalent to booing) when Morocco's Khalid Skah did his victory lap and when he was later presented the gold medal for winning the 10,000 meters?

A. They believed Skah had been illegally aided when a lapped teammate helped pace him; B. They believed Skah had elbowed another runner; C. Skah had taken so much time on his victory lap that he held up the meet; D. Skah had refused to shake hands with the other medal winners

17. True or False. Skah actually was disqualified and was reinstated as champion only after the Moroccan delegation filed a protest to overturn the ruling.

18. Who was the East African runner who dueled with Skah but was outkicked and forced to settle for the silver medal?

A. Addis Abebe of Ethiopia; B. Haile Gebrselassie of Ethiopia; C. Richard Chelimo of Kenya; D. Dieter Baumann of Germany

19. In 1995 this man became the first to shatter the 8-minute barrier in the steeplechase, clocking 7:59.18.

A. Andres Garderud of Sweden; B. Bronislaw Malinowski of Poland; C. Moses Kiptanui of Kenya; D. Henry Rono of Kenya

20. Although Olympic glory eluded him, this colorful Briton ran a world record in the 10,000 meters in 1973 in London, running 27:30. (He later directed the London Marathon.)

A. Bill Adcocks; B. Brendan Foster; C. Ian Stewart; D. Dave Bedford

21. Although perhaps better known as a great road racer, his 27:08.23 world-record performances on the track at Berlin in 1989 brought the 27-minute barrier into "shootin range" for those who followed.

A. Arturo Barrios of Mexico; B. Herb Lindsay of the U.S.A.; C.

Richard Chelimo of Kenya; D. Yobes Ondieki of Kenya

22. When Finland's Lasse Viren fell in the Olympic 10,000-meter run at Munich in 1972, how did he respond?

A. Got up, regained the lead after several laps, and won in a world-record time; B. Got up, gradually worked his way back into the race, and eventually dove at the tape to win by less than two-tenths of a second; C. Sat on the infield with his head bowed in agonized disbelief; D. Writhed in pain until he was removed from the track on a stretcher

23. Another runner, a proven Olympic star, also tumbled to the track with Viren in the Munich 10,000—and didn't finish the race. Who was he?

A. Mohammed Gammoudi of Tunisia; B. Dave Bedford of Great Britain; C. Ron Clarke of Australia; D. Frank Shorter of the U.S.A.

24. Accused of "blood boosting" (which was not against Olympic rules in 1972) by some skeptics, Viren occasionally joked with persistent journalists that his successes were due to:

A. Downing a six-pack of beer in a sauna after hard workouts; B. Special blood-red oranges, imported from Spain, meticulously hand-squeezed into fresh juice; C. Red currant juice laced with twice-distilled Finnish vodka; D. Reindeer milk

25. A silver medal winner at the Moscow Olympic 10,000 meters, this athlete (allegedly after a "religious awakening") admitted that he "blood-doped" prior to the 1980 Games.

26. True or False. Frank Shorter never won an NCAA title.

27. True or False. Kenyan steeplechasers swept all the medals in the men's 3000-meter steeplechase in both the 1992 Olympic Games and again at Athens in 2004. They are the only country to ever sweep this event.

28. When Bob Schul won the 5000-meter gold medal in the Tokyo Olympics, there were three men in the race who (at one time or another) held world records at various distances. Name them and their countries.

29. True or False. Bob Schul is the only American to ever win an Olympic gold medal in the 5000-meter run.

30. Paavo Nurmi's final gold medal (number nine!) of his glorious track career came in the 1928 Olympic Games in Amsterdam when he passed the defending 10,000-meter champ—his fellow Finn—in the final meters to clock an Olympic record of 30:18.

Who was the other guy?

31. Nurmi was often called "The Flying Finn" or "The Phantom Finn." What was the "other" Finn's nickname?

32. Paavo Nurmi often carried something in his hand while he raced. What was it?

A. a stopwatch; B. a four-leaf clover; C. a cross; D. a picture of his wife

33. When she won at Seoul in 1988—unleashing a blistering 31-second final 200!—this woman was the first to win an Olympic gold for the 10,000-meter run, a newly added event.

A. Ingrid Kristiansen of Norway; B. Olga Bondarenko of the Soviet Union; C. Lynn Jennings of the U.S.A.; D. Liz McColgan of Great Britain

34. Name the two African women who dueled for the 1992 10,000-meter Olympic gold and then thrilled the Barcelona crowd by taking a victory lap together.

35. He was the last American, as of 2005, to win an Olympic

medal in the 3000-meter steeplechase.

A. Henry Marsh; B. George Young; C. Mark Croghan; D. Brian Diemer

36. The medal-winning times in the 1932 Olympic steeplechase at Los Angeles were significantly slower than expected because:

A: The Santa Ana winds were kicking up gusts of 50 miles per hour during the event; B. The race was contested in a blinding rainstorm; C. Race officials mistakenly placed an extra set of barriers on the track; D. A substitute race official forgot to change the lap counter and the exhausted steeplechasers had to run an extra lap.

37. This American won a bronze medal in the 1932 steeplechase. He won 27 national titles in his career and also made the 1936 Olympic team.

A. Archie San Romani; B. Louis Zamperini; C. Joe McCluskey; D. Don Lash

38. True or False. Because of the controversy surrounding the 1932 Olympic steeplechase, officials considered rerunning the event the next day.

39. An elbowing incident led to the disqualification of Great

Britain's Christopher Brasher in the 1956 Melbourne Olympic Games. But Brasher was eventually reinstated when:

A. Race officials—using this option for the first time in Olympic history—reviewed films of the event; B. The British team officials promptly filed a protest and threatened to withdraw their entire team for the rest of the track-and-field events; C. The second- and third-place finishers assured race officials that Brasher's actions were slight and had no effect of the outcome of the race; D. Officials realized they had mistaken Brasher for British steeple teammate John Disley, who had finished sixth.

40. Announcer Bill Henry had to implore the fired-up American crowd to "Please remember, folks, these people are our guests!" when Finland's Lauri Lehtinen swerved back and forth on the homestretch to prevent this man from passing him in the 1932 Los Angeles Olympic 5000.

A. Archie San Romani; B. Ralph Hill; C. Louis Zamperini; D. Don Lash

41. He's the only man to win four straight NCAA 10,000-meter titles.

A. Steve Prefontaine of Oregon; B. Gerry Lindgren of Washington State; C. Suleiman Nyambui of Texas-El Paso; D. Henry Rono of Washington State; E. Ed Eyestone of Brigham Young

42. He's the current American-record holder for 5000 meters, as of September 2005.

A. Adam Goucher; B. Bob Kennedy; C. Sydney Maree; D. Meb Keflezighi

43. An FBI man in "real life," this former Penn State runner won the 1952 Olympic steeplechase over favorite Vladimir Kazantsev of the Soviet Union—and broke Kazantsev's world record in the process.

A. Horace Ashenfelter; B. Browning Ross; C. Charlie Maguire; D. Fred Wilt

44. He's the only steeplechaser to win two Olympic golds in that event.

A. Julius Kariuki of Kenya; B. Bronislaw Malinowski of Poland; C. Ville Ritola of Finland; D. Volmari Iso-Hollo of Finland

45. One of the top steeplechasers in the world for three straight Olympic Games, this two-time medal winner died in a car crash in 1981.

46. This Kenyan runner was the first man to crack 27 minutes for 10,000 meters.

A. Henry Rono; B. Yobes Ondieki; C. John Ngugi; D. Paul Tergat

47. Name the last American, as of 2005, to win an Olympic medal for 10,000 meters.

48. This Washington State runner won three NCAA titles in both the 5000 and 10,000 meters.

A. Henry Rono; B. Gerry Lindgren; C. John Ngeno; D. Dan Murphy

49. She was the first woman to break 31 minutes in the 10,000-meter run, clocking 30:59 in 1985.

A. Greta Waitz of Norway; B. Olga Bondarenko of Russia; C. Liz McColgan of Great Britain; D. Ingrid Kristiansen of Norway

50. SILVER-MEDAL QUESTION. Although some would say it's a controversial mark, only one woman in the world has broken 30 minutes for 10,000 meters. Name this world-record holder and her country.

51. She has the three fastest 3000-meter steeplechase times ever run by a woman—including the world record that's less than 2 seconds off cracking the 9-minute barrier.

A. Alesya Turova of Bulgaria; B. Jertum Kiptum of Kenya; C. Gulnara Samitova of Russia; D. Dorcus Inzikuru of Uganda

52. The first woman to win an NCAA title in the 3000-meter steeplechase was:

A. Lynn Jennings of Princeton; B. Brianna Shook of Toledo; C. Elizabeth Jackson of Brigham Young; D. Sonia O'Sullivan of Villanova

53. In May 2002, at the Stanford Cardinal Invitational in Palo Alto, California, fans chanted her first name for more than the final mile as this runner became the first American woman to run a sub-5-minute-per-mile pace for 10,000 meters, clocking 30:50.32. Name her and the person whose U.S. record she broke.

54. At the same meet in 2001, this U.S. man broke the American record for 10,000 meters with 27:13.98—a mark that had stood for nearly 15 years. Who's the man?

A. Alan Culpepper; B. Bob Kennedy; C. Meb Keflezighi; D. Todd Williams

55. The previous mark (27:20.56), set in 1986 in Brussels, Belgium, was held by this former University of Kentucky runner. Name him.

56. In 1999 this "Down Under" runner snipped two seconds off Ron Clarke's long-standing Australian record for 5000 meters, clocking 13:14. Name him.

A. Steve Moneghetti; B. Brian Lenton; C. Shaun Creighton; D. Lee Troop

57. Approximately how many decades and years had Clarke's national record (and a former world record) held up?

A. one decade and nine years; B. two decades and three years; C. two decades and seven years; D. three decades and three years

58. The Australian mark is now under 13 minutes and the man who ran it is only one of three runners not from an African country to ascend to that elite unit of 5000-meter "royalty," as of 2005. Name these three runners and their countries.

59. This Australian went on to be a top coach "Down Under"— but he did his collegiate running at the University of Houston and

twice won the NCAA title in the 3 mile in the early 1960s.

A. Allan Lawrence; B. Percy Cerutty; C. Pat Clohessy; D. Dave Power

60. There is very strong evidence that the same guy gave an American runner some important training advice in the year before the Tokyo Olympic Games—advice that perhaps helped with the American runner's success there. Who was the recipient of that advice from the Aussie?

A. Jim Ryun; B. Billy Mills; C. Bob Schul; D. Bill Dellinger

61. True or False. John Ngugi of Kenya was an outstanding cross-country runner, but he never won a major title on the track.

62. This talented and affable African runner—a future Olympic champ and world-record setter—was inspired to train for big things after listening on the radio to Miruts Yifter's great races in Moscow.

A. Haile Gebrselassie of Ethiopia; B. Kenenisa Bekele of Ethiopia; C. Hicham El Guerrouj of Morocco; D. Paul Tergat of Kenya

63. In what events did Yifter win gold medals at Moscow?

64. What was Yifter's rhyming nickname?

65. What amazing feat did the Ethiopian long-distance women accomplish at the 2005 IAAF World Track & Field Championships held in Helsinki, Finland?

66. The name of this current world-record holder in the men's steeplechase—first, middle, and last—begins with three S's . . . Who is he and what country does he represent?

67. As a college freshman, this runner set new U.S. junior (19 or under) marks in the 3000, 5000 and 10,000-meter runs.

A. Adam Goucher; B. Alan Webb; C. Galen Rupp; D. Dathan Ritzenhein

68. The previous holder of the 3000 and 5000-meter U.S. junior marks was:

A. Jim Ryun; B. Bob Kennedy; C. Gerry Lindgren; D. Steve Prefontaine

69. True or False. The 3000 and 5000-meter marks just broken

dated back to the mid-1960s.

70. The previous holder of the U.S. junior 10,000-meter mark was this former University of Oregon standout:

A. Alberto Salazar; B. Kenny Moore; C. Rudy Chapa; D. Steve Prefontaine

71. True or False. The 10,000-meter U.S. junior mark stood for more than a quarter of a century.

72. Coincidently, on the same day the 10,000-meter men's junior mark was broken, this Harvard freshman broke the women's 10,000-meter junior record (by just over 1 second), clocking 32:51.20 in New York City, while finishing second in the Ivy League Championship race. Name her and the Columbia runner who beat her by about 7 seconds.

73. The old women's junior mark for 10,000 meters was set in the late 1970s by this North Carolina State runner.

A. Mary Shea; B. Betty Jo Springs; C. Julie Shea; D. Suzie Tuffey

74. Only two men in NCAA Division I history have won three steeplechase titles. Name them.

A. Dan Lincoln (Arkansas) and James Munyala (Texas-El Paso); B. Henry Rono (Washington State) and Doug Brown (Tennessee); C. Mark Croghan (Ohio State) and Brian Diemer (Michigan); D. Doug Brown (Tennessee) and Marc Davis (Arizona)

75. His sizzling 8:12.39 remains the NCAA Division I men's steeplechase record.

A. Henry Rono of Washington State; B. Tim Broe of Alabama; C. Mark Croghan of Ohio State; D. Doug Brown of Tennessee

76. Hayward Field fanatics often wore GO PRE! T-shirts to show their support. There were also STOP PRE T-shirts. What did Prefontaine once do as a joke after winning a big race?

77. Who was the British runner who came on strong to nip a near-stumbling Prefontaine for the 1972 Olympic bronze medal in the last few meters? He also was an accomplished cross-country runner.

A. Ian Stewart; B. Brendan Foster; C. Frank Clement; D. Dave Moorcroft

78. On the 30th anniversary of Steve Prefontaine's death in a car crash (May 30, 1975), this Nike co-founder narrated a television ad (a rarity) in the Oregon star's honor.

A. Tom Jordan; B. Bill Bowerman; C. Kenny Moore; D. Phil Knight

79. "Pre" is honored by a road race and a small memorial museum in his hometown of:

A. Portland, Oregon; B. Medford, Oregon; C. Coos Bay, Oregon; D. Seaside, Oregon

80. In June 2005 this man set a new American record for the two-mile, blasting 8:11.48.

A. Alan Webb; B. Tim Broe; C. Adam Goucher; D. Galen Rupp

81. The new record shaved a scant 0.11 off the old mark, held by:

A. Jim Ryun; B. Bob Kennedy; C. Steve Scott; D. Steve Prefontaine

82. What is the translation of *Makata Taka Hela*—Billy Mill's Lakota (Sioux) name?

A. "he who loves his country" or "he who loves the earth"; B. "the warrior in flight"; C. "charges with courage"; D. "wild mountain horse"

83. Fittingly, Billy Mills's public speaking/inspirational publishing company is named this.

84. In addition to his famous Olympic race, Mills also set a world record for 6 miles in 1965, cranking out 27:11.6. In that race Mills (declared the winner by inches) finished in a virtual tie with this distance standout.

A. Jim Ryun; B. Gerry Lindgren; C. Ron Clarke; D. George Young

85. In addition to his major win at his best distance at the 1964 Olympics, Billy Mills also ran another event and placed 14th overall. What event?

A. 5000 meters; B. 3000 meter steeplechase; C. the marathon; D. 1500 meters

86. A former NCAA steeplechase champ, and several-time U.S. cross-country 4-K champ, this man broke the U.S. indoor 3000-meter record in 2002—clocking 7:39.23.

A. Adam Goucher; B. Tim Broe; C. Alan Culpepper; D. Steve Slattery

87. That time was less than a second faster than the mark set by this guy—better known as a great miler.

A. Alan Webb; B. Jim Beatty; C. Steve Scott; D. Dick Buerkle

88. When this Australian runner broke the 3-mile world record (13:10.8) at Dublin's Santry track in 1958, dozens and dozens in the crowd mobbed him, saying: "Let me touch you for luck, lad!"

A. Albie Thomas; B. John Landy; C. Ron Clarke; D. Dave Powers

89. How close did Kip Keino come to winning a second gold medal at the 1968 Olympic Games? He competed in the 5000-meter run.

A. 1 second; B. 2 seconds; C. only 0.5 second; D. just 0.2 second

90. What runner from Africa beat Keino in that race?

A. Naftali Temu, his teammate from Kenya; B. Mamo Wolde of Ethiopia; C. Mohammed Gammoudi of Tunisia; D. Miruts Yifter of Ethiopia

91. When Keino took up the steeplechase, he admitted his form over the barriers was less than perfect. What place did he get in the

1972 Olympic steeplechase in Munich?

A. first; B. second; C. third; D. he didn't make the final

92. This U.S. steeplechaser made four Olympic teams, and his 8:09.17—after two decades—remains the American record.

A. Farley Gerber; B. Henry Marsh; C. George Young; D. Brian Diemer

93. This gardener from Belgium once set a world record in the 5000-meter run (13:13.0), but his Olympic medal came in the 10,000 meters, chasing the Lasse Viren in 1972. Who was this Belgian runner?

A. Gaston Reiff; B. Emil Puttemans; C. Karel Lismont; D. Gaston Roelants

94. The 1976 men's Olympic 5000 was so competitive that less than 3 seconds separated first from seventh. As Lasse Viren fought off New Zealanders Dick Quax and Rod Dixon, this West German runner dove at the line to snag third (over Dixon) and the bronze medal. Who was he?

A. Thomas Wessinghage; B. Bodo Tummler; C. Klaus-Peter Hildenbrand; D. Harald Norpoth

95. En route to what was then a new Olympic Games 5000-meter record (13:05), this runner unleashed a 55-second last lap—and waved to the crowd in the final meters while he was doing it. In his prime that day, he was only about 5 seconds off Dave Moorcroft's world record.

A. Said Aouita of Morocco; B. Moses Tanui of Kenya; C. Alberto Cova of Italy; D. Yobes Ondieki of Kenya

96. He was one of the few men to beat Emil Zatopek in the 1948, but he had to set an Olympic record in the 5000 meters to do it. His margin of victory? Just two-tenths of a second!

A. Alain Mimoun of France; B. Gaston Reiff of Belgium; C. Christopher Chataway of Great Britain; D. Gordon Pirie of Great Britain

97. Using his miler's speed, this runner nailed down a gold medal in the inaugural world championship 5000-meter race in 1983. It went a long way to reducing some of the pain of twice missing Olympic medals by one place.

A. Marcus O'Sullivan of Ireland; B. Mark Nenow of the U.S.A.; C. Eamonn Coghlan of Ireland; D. Henry Marsh of the U.S.A.

DISTANCE ACES
ANSWERS

1. A
2. Gundar Hägg of Sweden
3. C
4. C
5. Lewis Tewanima
6. B
7. Fernando Mamede of Portugal
8. Emil Zatopek of Czech gave Ron Clarke of Australia one of his gold medals.
9. C
10. B
11. C
12. C
13. A. Boersen finished in 31 minutes and change, and actually took more time off his PR than Clarke did off his in clocking the world record.
14. D
15. B
16. A. Hammou Botayeb, Skah's Moroccan teammate (who was being lapped), tried to help pace the eventual winner. Skah later vehemently declared that he told Botayeb to go away—he didn't need anyone's help.
17. True

18. C
19. C
20. D
21. A
22. A
23. A
24. D
25. Kaarlo Maaninka of Finland
26. False. Shorter won the 1969 6-mile outdoor crown his senior year.
27. False. The Finns (1928) and the Swedes (1948) swept all the steeplechase medals, too.
28. Ron Clarke of Australia, Harald Norpoth of West Germany, Michel Jazy of France
29. True. But Ralph Hill in '32 came as close as you can get without doing it.
30. Ville Ritola
31. Ritola was sometimes called "The Flying Wolf."
32. A
33. B
34. Derartu Tulu of Ethiopia, gold, and Elana Meyer of South Africa, silver
35. D
36. D
37. C. McCluskey actually had the silver medal clinched, but when the runners were mistakenly asked to run an extra lap, Briton Thomas Evenson passed him and nipped him at the line.
38. True
39. C
40. B
41. C. 1979-1982

42. B
43. A
44. D
45. Bronislaw Malinowski of Poland
46. B
47. Lynn Jennings
48. B
49. D
50. Wang Junxia of China
51. C
52. C
53. Deena Drossin and Lynn Jennings
54. C
55. Mark Nenow
56. D
57. D
58. Craig Mottram of Australia; Bob Kennedy of the U.S.A.;
Dieter Bauman of Germany
59. C
60. B
61. False. Ngugi was the Olympic 10,000-meter champion in
1988 at Seoul.
62. A
63. The 5000 and the 10,000 meters
64. "Yifter the Shifter"
65. They swept all the medals in both the 5000 and 10,000-
meter races.
66. Saif Saeed Shaheen of Quatar
67. C
68. C
69. True

70. C
71. True
72. Lindsey Scherf of Harvard finished second to Columbia's Caroline Bierbaum.
73. A
74. A. Lincoln won 2001-2003; Munyala 1975-1977.
75. A
76. He put on a STOP PRE! T-shirt for his victory lap.
77. A
78. D
79. C
80. A
81. B
82. A
83. 10-K Gold
84. B
85. C
86. B
87. C
88. A
89. D. It was less than 2 yards
90. C
91. A
92. B
93. B
94. C
95. A
96. B
97. C

MARATHON

Emil Zatopek didn't run very many marathons, but he seemed able to sum up the experience quite readily. "We are different, in essence, than other men. If you want to win something, run 100 meters," Emil once quipped. "But if you want to experience something, run a marathon."

What we experience, of course, can be anything from brilliance to blisters, euphoria to our very own disaster wrapped up in a 26.2-mile package.

The marathon can fool you. Italy's Gelindo Bordin—who had a luminous marathon career—had a relatively easy, pain-free first marathon experience. He won his debut in Milan in 2:13:30 and admitted: "I said to myself, 'If this is the marathon, it's no problem.' That's the only marathon I ever said that about."

The marathon can hurt you, if you actually race it. "To describe the agony of the marathon to someone who's never run it is like trying to explain color to someone who was born blind," said Boston Marathon winner Jerome Drayton of Canada.

The marathon can humble you, stated marathon great Bill Rodgers. And certainly he'd get no argument from John J. Kelley, one of his predecessors in the sport, who spoke eloquently about his "blow-up" at his debut Yonkers Marathon in 1954.

"Despite the sun and the caution it should have instilled in me, I wanted to prove the course wasn't that bad. But by 22 miles I got the whoozies and pretty soon I'm sitting on a rock, and the next thing I know I'm in the car. Fifteen minutes pass, and Nick Costes walks up to the car and climbs in. So these two heroes are out. We sit there like melted butter. Ted Corbitt just trudged along and won with a 2:46:13. Only forgetfulness and the indestructibility of youth brought me back to that race again."

But the marathon could also—in its strange way—offer redemption. Kelley not only came back to win Yonkers, but also captured the 1957 Boston Marathon.

With so much potential for both glory and abject defeat, it's no wonder that the marathon can produce so many great moments—and therefore trivia questions—to those who follow the sport. The records . . . the runs for Olympic fame . . . the infamous collapses and near collapses . . . it's all there in one event.

With the world record for the marathon now just slightly under 2 hours and 5 minutes, it's becoming increasingly impossible to ignore what is perhaps the next big challenge in distance running. If Bannister's sub-4-minute mile was equated with scaling Mount Everest, then what can one possibly say about the 2-hour marathon? One might make a case that the sub-2-hour marathon would be the equivalent to putting a man on the moon, or maybe Mars, for that matter.

In Hugh Atkinson's novel *The Games* fictional coach Bill Persons alludes to the elusive dream. "The two-hour marathon. The thing that can't be done. The mark they talk about in whispers."

In real life, Australian marathoner Derek Clayton is on the record as a non-believer.

"I think the idea of a two-hour marathon is thoroughly ridiculous," said Clayton. "Absolutely ridiculous. I cannot foresee, *ever,* anyone breaking two hours."

But Clayton's words were uttered more than 25 years ago, long before they broke 2:05 at Berlin. If someone runs, say, 2:03, talk of a 2-hour marathon will no longer be conducted in mere whispers.

1. The marathon gets its name from:

A Greek word meaning "endurance"; B. The battlefield site of a critical Greek victory over the Persians in 490 BC; C. A town in England, starting place of the 1908 London Olympic race; D. A Greek word meaning "stupidity"

2. In 1896 he won the first marathon—a 25-miler from Stamford, Connecticut, to New York City—ever run in the United States.

A. John J. McDermott; B. Ronald McDonald; C. Tom Longboat; D. Fred Lorz

3. The first Boston Marathon began in Ashland, Massachusetts, a starting line scratched across a dirt road. The field consisted of 18 men, 10 of whom finished. Who finished first in this 1897 inaugural event?

A. Hamilton Gray of New York; B. John J. McDermott of New York; C. Ronald McDonald of Canada; D. Dick Grant of Harvard

4. The marathon is 26 miles and how many yards long?

A. 26 yards; B. 440 yards (approximately one lap on the stadium track); C. 365 yards; D. 385 yards

5. The first marathon run at this 26.2-mile distance was:

A: The Athens Olympics in 1896; B. The Boston Marathon in 1897; C. The 1924 Olympic Games in Paris; D. The 1908 London Olympic Games

6. The 1908 Olympic Marathon finished in the Olympic Stadium in Shepherd's Bush, but it began at what famous British landmark?

A. Stonehenge; B. Buckingham Palace; C. Windsor Castle; D. The White Cliffs of Dover

7. Dorando Pietri of Italy was disqualified from the 1908 Olympic Marathon because:

A. He interfered with another runner; B. He received water from his coaches, which was against the rules; C. He cut the course; D. Officials helped him across the finish line after he collapsed on the stadium track

8. The man who won the Olympic gold medal because of Pietri's misfortune was:

A. John Hayes of the U.S.A.; B. Tom Longboat of Canada; C. Charles Hefferon of South Africa; D. James Lightbody of the U.S.A.

9. Dorando Pietri pulled away from Hayes in the final mile of a professional, mano-a-mano marathon held in New York City in November 1908, setting a world record of 2 hours, 44 minutes. Where was it held?

A. The Polo Grounds; B. Ebbet's Field in Brooklyn; C. Central Park; D. Madison Square Garden

10. A waiter from London, who stood all of 4 feet 11 inches, upset Pietri, Hayes, and famed Englishman Alfred Shrubb (among others) in a professional marathon at the Polo Grounds, in April 1909. Who was he?

A. Willie Shoemaker; B. Tom Longboat; C. Henri St. Yves; D. Keith Richards

11. SILVER-MEDAL QUESTION While Kenneth McArthur and Christian Gitsham (the gold and silver 1912 Olympic marathon medal winners) celebrated in the streets of Stockholm, this marathoner lay in a nearby room, delirious from the effects of heatstroke that had forced him to drop out of the race. A three-time national marathon champ of Portugal, he died the next day.

12. Her 3-hour, 40-minute, 22-second marathon effort at Chiswick, England in 1926 is generally regarded as the first official marathon time for women.

A. Maggie Thatcher; B. Emily Brontë; C. Vanessa Redgrave; D. Violet Piercy

13. This country has won the most Olympic medals (gold, silver, bronze totaled) in the men's marathon.

A. The U.S.A.; B. Great Britain; C. Finland; D. Ethiopia

14. Before Khalid Khannouchi was granted American citizenship, this man—a former Ivy League runner—held the U.S. record in the marathon.

A. Frank Shorter; B. Bill Rodgers; C. Bob Kempainen; D. Meb Keflezighi

15. A historic "battle royal" among three of the sport's greatest distance runners occurred in the 2002 London Marathon, with the winner clocking a world record of 2:05:38—including one of

track's "kings" making his marathon debut. Name those three men.

16. A Mexican and a German runner (male and female, respectively) are the only runners to win three straight London Marathon titles. Pick the right pair!

A. Salvador Garcia and Uta Pippig; B. Arturo Barrios and Uta Pippig; C. Rodolfo Gomez and Charlotte Teske; D. Dionicio Ceron and Katrin Dorre

17. She ran some of her very best races after turning 40, finishing second to world-record holder Ingrid Kristiansen at London in 1987 (2:26 and change!) and then winning the New York City Marathon (at age 42) that fall in 2:30.

A. Priscilla Welch of Great Britain; B. Carla Beurskens of the Netherlands; C. Jacqueline Gareau of Canada; D. Ivy Palm of Sweden

18. He was the first master (40-plus years old) to break 2:10 in the marathon.

A. Andres Espinosa of Mexico; B. Jack Foster of New Zealand; C. John Campbell of New Zealand; D. Bill Rodgers of the U.S.A.

19. A wrong turn almost cost this man the 1994 New York City Marathon title, but one of NYC's finest redirected him and he rallied to beat Mexico's Benjamin Parades by just 2 seconds in 2:11.21.

A. Gianni Poli of Italy; B. Ibrahim Hussein of Kenya; C. Paul Evans of Great Britain; D. German Silva of Mexico

20. Who was the first runner from an African country to win the Olympic marathon gold medal?

A: Ken McArthur of South Africa; B. Abebe Bikila of Ethiopia; C. Mamo Wolde of Ethiopia; D. Douglas Wakiihuri of Kenya

21. The great Finnish runner Paavo Nurmi was considered a favorite to win the 1932 Olympic Marathon in Los Angeles, but it never happen because:

A. he tore his Achilles tendon a week before the race; B. he caught the flu and could not train; C. he was suspended from amateur competition one week before the Games began for alleged expense money violations; D. he dropped out of the race 8 eight miles

22. What day of the week is the Boston Marathon typically held?

A. Monday; B. Friday; C. Saturday; D. Sunday

23. In the final miles, the Boston Marathon course runs by what famous Beantown landmark?

A. The Boston Garden; B. The Bunker Hill Memorial; C. Boston Common; D. Fenway Park

24. In the 15 years from 1991 to 2005, Kenyan men have scored how many Boston Marathon victories?

A. 15; B. 10; C. 8; D. 13

25. A conscientious objector to the Vietnam War, this 1973 Boston Marathon winner spent time (when he wasn't training!) washing dishes in a hospital.

A. Amby Burfoot; B. Bill Rodgers; C. George A. Custer; D. Jon Anderson

26. This Canadian runner won the 1914 Boston Marathon (and allegedly asked for a cigarette as soon as he crossed the line!) but died in action storming a German position in Belgium the next year.

A. Edouard Fabre; B. Tom Longboat; C. Gerard Cote; D. Jimmy Duffy

27. With temperatures flirting with 100 degrees for much of the race, the 1976 Boston Marathon took on what nickname?

A. "Steam Bath Boston"; B. "Baked Beantown"; C. "The Run for the Hoses"; D. "The Duel in the Sun"

28. Name the former Georgetown runner who won that 1976 blazing-hot Boston Marathon.

A. John Gregorek; B. Steve Stageberg; C. Jack Fultz; D. John Trautmann

29. He was the first college undergraduate since 1898 to win the Boston Marathon.

A. Jon Anderson; B. Amby Burfoot; C. Neil Cusack; D. Jerome Drayton

30. "Heartbreak Hill" got its name from famed *Boston Globe* sportwriter Jerry Nason in the 1936 duel between what two great Boston Marathon runners?

A. Clarence DeMar and Johnny Miles of Canada; B. Ellison "Tarzan" Brown and John A. Kelley; C. Clarence DeMar and Olympic champ Albin Stenroos of Finland; D. Tom Longboat of

Canada and Olympic champ Johnny Hayes

31. In the ill-fated Moscow Olympic boycott year, he won the 1980 U.S. Olympic Marathon Trials from Buffalo to Niagara Falls, Canada, after a near miss in 1976.

A. Tony Sandoval; B. Bill Rodgers; C. Jeff Wells; D. Benji Durden

32. After his Boston Marathon victory (in which he beat the reigning Olympic champion from Finland), he preached in a Boston church and lectured to the congregation that "There is no secret to this marathon game. You must think clean, live clean, obey the laws of nature and God."

A. Johnny Miles; B. Jeff Wells; C. Clarence DeMar; D. Jimmy Duffy

33. A former world-class marathoner for Canada (third in the 1977 Boston Marathon), a coach at UC Berkeley, this founder of the PowerBar company died suddenly in 2004. Who was he?

34. Often known for rabbit-like starts in big races, this free-spirited guy led the 1980 U.S. Marathon Trials for 15 miles, wearing a T-shirt that prophetically read: THE ROAD TO MOSCOW ENDS HERE. (Hint: He was one of the lost "Blues Brothers.")

A. Gary Fanelli; B. Tom Byers; C. Paul Pilkington; D. Don Kardong

35. This Utah-based runner once "stole" the 1994 Los Angeles Marathon by refusing to drop out after he hit his "splits" as pacesetter and turned "killer rabbit."

A. Henry Marsh; B. Paul Pilkington; C. Paul Cummings; D. Ed Eyestone

36. He's the only man to win Japan's prestigious Fukuoka Marathon four years in a row. (Hint: The "second best" choice also has four career Fukuoka wins, but not consecutive ones!)

A. Toshihiko Seko of Japan; B. Bill Rodgers of the U.S.A.; C. Frank Shorter of the U.S.A.; D. Jerome Drayton of Canada

37. This man tied with Frank Shorter at the 1972 Olympic Marathon Trials held in Eugene, Oregon, then narrowly missed a medal in the Olympic Games.

A. Ron Daws; B. Jack Bacheler; C. Kenny Moore; D. Don Kardong

38. Of these four famous marathon "collapses" (or near collapses),

which runner managed to somehow cross the finish line without assistance?

A. Gabriele Andersen-Scheiss of Switzerland (1984 Olympic Marathon in Los Angeles); B. Jim Peters of Great Britain (the British Empire Games in Vancouver, BC, in 1954); C. Francisco Lazaro of Portugal (1912 Olympic Marathon in Stockholm); D. Dorando Pietri of Italy (1908 Olympic Marathon in London)

39. What multi-time Boston Marathon winner took a number of years off during his career (before returning to win the race several times) because doctors convinced him running marathons might be dangerous to his heart?

A. Ellison "Tarzan" Brown; B. Bill Rodgers; C. John A. Kelley; D. Clarence DeMar

40. In addition to winning a gold medal, what were two other noteworthy things about Abebe Bikila's marathon win in the 1960 Rome Olympics?

41. A bronze-medal winner in the 1964 Tokyo Olympic marathon, what tragic fate awaited Japan's Kokichi Tsuburaya?

42. Tripped up by a rope that was used to hold back runners at the start, this world-class runner "rolled through" and bounced back up

to finish sixth in the 1987 Boston Marathon. (Hint: He had charged to a course record in a previous Boston.)

A. Arturo Barrios of Mexico; B. Bill Rodgers of the U.S.A.; C. Toshihiko Seko of Japan; D. Rob de Castella of Australia

43. Miffed at officials who demanded they start 10 minutes ahead of the men, women marathoners staged a starting-line protest at what event?

A. The 1968 Boston Marathon; B. The 1972 New York City Marathon; C. The 1984 Olympic Marathon in Los Angeles; D. The 1936 Olympic Marathon in Berlin

44. She was the first woman to break the formidable 2-hour, 20-minute barrier in the marathon.

A. Tegla Larope of Kenya; B. Paula Radcliffe of Great Britain; C. Ingrid Kristiansen of Norway; D. Naoko Takihashi of Japan

45. The 1980 Boston Marathon was noteworthy because:

A. of a bizarre cheating scandal; B. Bill Rodgers won his fourth (and final) Boston Marathon title; C. Jacqueline Gareau of Canada set a women's course record; D. All of the above

46. In 1980 Boston Marathon finishers received yogurt and energy bars for the first time. Prior to that, the postrace nourishment for runners was:

A. two large cornmeal pancakes with maple syrup; B. beef stew; C. cabbage and noodles; D. a bagel and cup of hot tea with honey

47. If someone "pulls a Rosie Ruiz" in a marathon, they've done what?

A. Missed the start of the race; B. Hit "the wall" just yards from the finish line and crawled in; C. Cheated by cutting the course; D. Dropped out after establishing a huge lead

48. Briton Paula Radcliffe's current world record in the women's marathon is 2 hours, 15 minutes, 25 seconds, run at London on April 13, 2003. What else was noteworthy about her run?

A. She finished eighth overall in the race; B. She beat all the British men in the race; C. She stopped to tie a loose shoelace three times; D. Her splits were virtually dead even . . . 1:07:43 for the first half, 1:07:42 for the second half; E. All of the above

49. In 1963 this American set what was then the world record in Chiswick, England, clocking 2 hours, 14 minutes, 28 seconds—but finished sixth in the Olympic Marathon a year later.

A. Ellison "Tarzan" Brown; B. Leonard "Buddy" Edelen; C. Hal Higdon; D. John J. Kelley

50. In the space of a year (1969-1970) this man won four major marathons—including the European Championships in hilly Athens, the Commonweath Games Marathon in Edinburgh, Scotland, in 2:09:28, and the Boston Marathon in a then course record of 2:10:30—and finished second in another at Fukuoka in Japan. (Hint: He was also famous for his innovative designs for better racing wear and an incredibly long training streak.)

A. Ian Thompson of Great Britain; B. Ron Hill of Great Britain; C. Derek Clayton of Australia; D. Jerome Drayton of Canada

51. Who was the first men's Olympic Marathon champion to win the Boston Marathon?

A. Abebe Bikila of Ethiopia; B. Gelindo Bordin of Italy; C. Frank Shorter of the U.S.A.; D. Rob de Castella of Australia

52. Three women have won Boston Marathon titles and Olympic Marathon gold medals. Name them.

53. Although she wasn't an official entry, this woman seems to have been the first finisher of the Boston Marathon when she clocked 3:21:40 in 1966.

A. Roberta Gibb; B. Kathrine Switzer; C. Nina Kuscsik; D. Doris Brown Heritage

54. This woman ran with the first official number in 1967—and finished—despite the fact that an enraged race official attempted to tear the number off her during the race. Name her.

55. Name that race official, famous for his Scottish "burr" and his love for the Boston Marathon.

56. He's the only man to win the New York City Marathon four years in a row.

A. Orlando Pizzolata of Italy; B. Bill Rodgers; C. John Kagwe of Kenya; D. Tom Fleming

57. "A miler's kick does the trick!" was the mantra this man repeated to himself as he chased down Englishman Geoff Smith to win the 1983 New York City Marathon in dramatic fashion and a sub-2:09 clocking.

A. Alberto Salazar of the U.S.A.; B. Bill Rodgers of the U.S.A.; C. Eamonn Coghlan of Ireland; D. Rod Dixon of New Zealand

58. The New York City Marathon course through the five boroughs was first run in what year?

A: 1969; B. 1972; C. 1976; D. 1981

59. Which of these Olympic marathon champions won the gold medal in the city of his or her birth?

A. Thomas Hicks of the U.S.A. at St. Louis in 1904; B. Joan Benoit Samuelson of the U.S.A. in Los Angeles in 1984; C. Carlos Lopes of Portugal in Los Angeles in 1984; D. Frank Shorter of the U.S.A. in Munich in 1972

60. At the finish of the 1904 Olympic Marathon in St. Louis, Fred Lorz of New York was photographed with Alice Roosevelt, daughter of the president, and nearly awarded the gold medal. But he was suddenly disqualified when it was discovered that:

A. He was given doses of strychnine and brandy throughout the race to combat pain; B. He inadvertently ran the wrong way on the track as he entered the stadium; C. He had hitched a ride in a car for 11 miles and then began running again; D. he had placed a large wager on the outcome of the race

61. Fred Lorz later redeemed himself (after a "lifetime ban" was lifted) by:

A. winning the 1908 Olympic Marathon in London; B. winning the 1905 Boston Marathon; C. winning an ultramarathon race across the United States; D. winning a marathon race staged on Madison Square Garden's indoor wooden track

62. In the 1907 Boston Marathon, what happened that cost many in the field more than a minute in time in the first half of the race?

A. A farmer's wagon broke down in the middle of the course, scattering chickens all over the road; B. There was an accident involving three automobiles; C. The Framingham Police Department stopped the marathon because race officials failed to get a permit; D. A freight train cut off the field briefly as it rambled through Framingham

63. This Canadian runner, who avoided the above mishap, went on to set what was then a course record for the Boston Marathon. His name was:

A. Johnny Miles; B. Tom Longboat; C. Gerard Cote; D. Jerome Drayton

64. How many times did Norway's Grete Waitz win the New York City Marathon?

A. 4; B. 6; C. 9; D. 12

65. Who was the first woman to break 3 hours in the Boston Marathon?

A. Nina Kuscsik; B. Joan Benoit Samuelson; C. Kathrine Switzer; D. Michiko Gorman

66. Approximately how many people ran in Boston on April 15, 1996—the Centennial Celebration of the famed marathon?

A. 3,800; B. 25,000; C. 35,000; D. 55,000

67. According to some reports, this winner of the 1896 Olympic Marathon in Athens was said to have downed a glass of wine from a roadside tavern during the race. His name was:

A. Edwin Flack of Australia; B. J. P. Bordeaux of France; C. Spiridon Louis of Greece; D. Dorando Pietri of Italy

68. Lisa Larsen Weidenbach, a former collegiate swimmer at Michigan who turned to running, won the Boston and Chicago Marathon titles in her career. But she also experienced "tough luck" when she:

A. Missed a bronze medal in the 1988 Olympic Games by just 3 seconds; B. Missed the turn for Central Park while leading the 1987 New York City Marathon; C. Missed making the U.S. Olympic Marathon team with fourth-place finishes in 1984, 1988, and 1992; D. Twisted her ankle and failed to finish while leading the 1990 Ironman Triathlon in Hawaii

69. Australia's Derek Clayton ran 2:08:33.6 (the first man to break 2:09) in 1969 to set a world record in the marathon. Whose record did he break?

A. Abebe Bikela's of Ethiopia; B. Basil Heatley's of Great Britain; C. Waldemar Cierpinski's of East Germany; D. Clayton broke his own record

70. In addition to other accomplishments, he was the first man to run under 2:12, 2:11 and 2:10 for the marathon.

A. Abebe Bikela of Ethiopia; B. Basil Heatley of Great Britain; C. Derek Clayton of Australia; D. Jerome Drayton of Canada

71. "God! He's running backwards!" were the words exclaimed by a broadcaster who witnessed the horrific collapse of this marathoner (a man who set the world record at that distance several times) in the 1954 British Empire Games held on a surprisingly hot day in Vancouver, British Columbia.

A. Jim Peters; B. Basil Heatley; C. Ron Hill; D. Ian Thompson

72. She started as a national-class 400-meter hurdler, but became a world-class distance runner, including an Olympic silver medal.

A. Lisa Martin Ondieki of Australia; B. Grete Waitz of Norway; C. Joyce Chepchumba of Kenya; D. Elana Meyer of South Africa

73. In the first-ever women's Olympic Marathon in Los Angeles in 1984, Joan Benoit Samuelson made her major move:

A: On a long, gradual hill just before the halfway mark; B. less than three miles into the race; C. at the 20-mile mark; D. just before entering the Olympic Stadium

74. Already having made the Olympic team in the 10,000-meter track race, this Florida Track Club member slowed up a step at the finish line to allow his friend/teammate Jack Bacheler to land the third and last slot in the marathon at Eugene, Oregon, in 1972. Who was he?

A. Jeff Galloway; B. Keith Brantly; C. Ron Daws; D. Benji Durden

75. Better known as a steeplechaser (he won an Olympic medal in that event), this man won the 1968 U.S. Olympic Marathon Trials (in his first marathon attempt) in the thin air of Alamosa, Colorado.

A. Horace Ashenfelter; B. Brian Deimer; C. George Young; D. Henry Marsh

76. In the 1992 women's U.S. Olympic Trials Marathon in Houston, slick road conditions and jostling at a water stop caused one of the front-runners, Janis Klecker, to fall to the pavement. Which rival marathoner ran back to dramatically assist Klecker to her feet?

A. Mary Decker Slaney; B. Joan Benoit Samuelson; C. Francie Larrieu-Smith; D. Cathy O'Brien

77. Which woman ended up winning the race in a time of 2:30:12, making her first U.S. Olympic team?

A. Francie Larrieu-Smith; B. Cathy O'Brien; C. Janis Klecker; D. Julie Isphording

78. In 1984 this young woman (just 16!) from New England set a new world junior marathon record (2:34:24) in Olympia, Washington, en route to a ninth-place finish.

A. Julie Shea; B. Blake Russell; C. Cathy Schiro; D. Lynn Jennings

79. She set a U.S. women's masters marathon mark at Chicago in 2003 in 2:32:39, but her most famous race was an upset (she was seeded 61st coming into the event!) win at the 1996 U.S. Olympic Marathon Trials in South Carolina.

A. Margaret Groos; B. Jenny Spangler; C. Chris Clark; D. Nancy Ditz

80. When she won the 1992 New York City Marathon in 2:27:33—her first-ever race at the 26.2-mile distance—this confident distance runner set a then world record for a "debut" marathon.

A. Olga Markova of the Soviet Union; B. Uta Pippig of Germany; C. Liz McColgan of Great Britain; D. Lynn Jennings of the U.S.

81. This local lad attended Tufts University in nearby Medford and represented the Boston Athletic Association. He pushed French Canadian Gerard Cote to a then course record (2:31:02) and fourth Boston title. But he also threatened to slug Cote because the veteran from Quebec stepped on the heels of his running shoes during their 1948 Boston Marathon duel.

A. John A. Kelley; B. Jesse Van Zant; C. Tom Crane; D. Ted Vogel

82. This colorful Boston Marathoner dove into Lake Cochituate in the early miles of the 1938 Boston Marathon to cool off on a hot day. He climbed back out, soaking wet, and went on to finish a modest 51st (but he came back to win Boston in 1939).

A. Les Pawson of Rhode Island; B. Ellison "Tarzan" Brown of

Rhode Island; C. Gerard Cote of Quebec; D. Clarence DeMar of Massachusetts

83. After an altercation with Nazi toughs in a bar brawl, this Boston Marathon champion was tossed in jail during the 1936 Olympic Games in Berlin.

A. John A. Kelley; B. Ellison "Tarzan" Brown; C. Les Pawson; D. Clarence DeMar

84. When won the 1957 Boston Marathon in a course record time of 2:20:05, he became the only Boston Athletic Association runner to win the BAA's own event. He also was the only American to win Boston between the years of 1945 and 1967.

A. John A. Kelley; B. Ellison "Tarzan" Brown; C. John J. Kelley; D. Les Pawson

85. She's the only woman to have finished four Olympic Marathons, including a medal-winning performance in Barcelona in 1992 and a fifth-place finish in Los Angeles in 1984.

A. Allison Roe of New Zealand; B. Ingrid Kristiansen of Norway; C. Rosa Mota of Portugal; D. Lorranie Moller of New Zealand

86. Grete Waitz set the world record for the women's marathon

four times in her career. The final time was on April 17, 1983, at the London Marathon, clocking 2:25:28.7. Her record lasted for:

A. one day; B. 6 months and 4 days; C. 4 years; D. 11 years

87. With eight career victories in the Honolulu Marathon, this Dutch woman is the undisputed Queen of the Islands.

A. Maria Gommers; B. Fanny Blankers-Koen; C. Carla Beurskens; D. Elly van Langen

88. Emil Zatopek had never run the marathon until he won his gold medal in the 1952 Helsinki Olympic Games, in what was then an Olympic record of 2:23:03. What other notable accomplishment (one that is still unequaled today) did this victory bring Zatopek?

A. He was the only man to lead start-to-finish in an Olympic marathon; B. It made him the only distance runner to win the historic "triple"—the 5000 meters, 10,000 meters, and marathon—all in the same Olympic Games; C. It was also a world record; D. It made Zatopek the first Czech athlete to win an Olympic medal in track

89. This Frenchman finished second to Zatopek so many times that he was nicknamed "the eternal second." But he won the 1956 Olympic Marathon in Melbourne, Australia, and was waiting at the line to greet the great Czech runner, who struggled home sixth.

A. Alain Mimoun; B. Jules Ladoumegue; C. Jean-Claude Killy; D. Guy Drut

90. His marathon win at the Antwerp Games made him the only Finn to snag Olympic gold medals in the 5000 meters, 10,000 meters and marathon—although he didn't win them all in the same Olympics.

A. Johannes "Hannes" Kolehmainen; B. Vilho "Ville" Ritola; C. Paavo Nurmi; D. Lasse Viren

91. Vanderlei de Lima of Brazil led the 2004 Athens Olympic Marathon for more than 20 miles before:

A. he was accidentally knocked down by a course marshal's bicycle; B. he was forced to stop with a severe case of leg cramps; C. he was inadvertently directed off course; D. he was tackled by a defrocked priest

92. De Lima's bronze-medal finish marked the first time a South American won a marathon medal since this man snagged a silver medal in 1952.

A. Reinaldo Gorno of Argentina; B. Ronaldo da Costa of Brazil; C. Miquel Plaza Reyes of Chile; D. Delfo Cabrera of Argentina

93. What demonstration of joy did de Lima exhibit as he entered the Panathinakio Stadium in Athens?

A: He did "the airplane"; B. He pumped his fist triumphantly in the air; C. He did a cartwheel on the track; D. He waved and gave the "peace sign" to the crowd

94. In addition to his medal, de Lima was also awarded this:

A. the Athenian Award for courage; B. the Pierre de Coubertin Award for sportsmanship; C. a replica of an ancient Olympic urn; D. a bronzed shoe worn by the first Olympic Marathon champ, Spiridon Louis of Greece

95. Almost lost in the excitement concerning de Lima's bizarre incident, this man charged to a course record in 2:10:55 and the 2004 Olympic Marathon gold.

A. Paul Tergat of Kenya; B. Stefano Baldini of Italy; C. Meb Keflezighi of the U.S.A.; D. Josia Thugwane of South Africa

96. In addition, the 2004 winner narrowly rewrote the Athens Marathon course record of 2:11:08, set way back in 1969 by this Olympic marathon runner.

A. Bill Adcocks of Great Britain; B. Basil Heatley of Great Britain; C. Ron Hill of Great Britain; D. Derek Clayton of Australia

97. Irish distance ace Eamonn Coghlan once called fourth in the Olympics "the absolutely worst place to finish . . ." This British marathon runner, twice fourth in Olympic competition, would probably concur.

A. Ron Hill; B. Brian Kilby; C. Jon Brown; D. Basil Heatley

98. John A. Kelley won two Boston Marathons and John J. Kelley won one. But how many second-place finishes (combined) did they have in that famous race?

A. six; B. nine; C. ten; D. a dozen

99. The marathon world-record holder in 1952 was Englishman Jim Peters. What place did he finish in the Helsinki Olympic Marathon?

A. Third, good for the bronze medal; B. Fourth by 2 seconds; C. Last; D. He did not finish

100. In the history of the marathon, this ranks as one of the top conversational moments: Who pulled up alongside the race leader—Jim Peters of Great Britain—and asked: "The pace, Jim . . . Is it too fast?"

A. Alain Mimoun of France; B. Tom Richards of Great Britain; C. Emil Zatopek of Czechoslovakia; D. Delfo Cabrea of Argentina, the defending champion

101. And Peters's famous reply?

102. In the history of the men's marathon, which runner set the world record a record four times?

A. Jim Peters of Great Britain; B. Abebe Bikila of Ethiopia; C. Derek Clayton of Australia; D. Paul Tergat of Kenya

103. Which country has won more Olympic medals in the marathon—Australia or New Zealand?

104. Only two men have been able to win an Olympic gold medal in the marathon and set a world (and Olympic) Record in the process. Name them.

A. Abebe Bikila of Ethiopia and Emil Zatopek of Czechoslovakia; B. Gelindo Bordin of Italy and Paavo Nurmi of Finland; C. Carlos Lopes of Portugal and Waldemar Cierpinski of East Germany; D. Abebe Bikila of Ethiopia and Johannes "Hannes" Kolehmainen of Finland

105. As of 2005, an American man has not won the Boston Marathon in more than:

A: 15 years; B. 22 years; C. 29 years; D. 32 years

106. The last American male to win the Boston Marathon (as of 2005) did his collegiate running in the Big Ten, at Michigan, then moved up to the marathon later in his career.

A. Greg Meyer; B. Garry Bjorklund; C. Craig Virgin; D. Steve Hoag

107. The last American woman to win the Boston Marathon title (as of 2005) was:

A. Allison Roe; B. Joan Benoit Samuelson; C. Lisa Larsen Weidenbach; D. Deena Drossin Kastor

108. On April 13, 2003, Deena Drossin Kastor broke Joan Benoit Samuelson's American record for the marathon by 5 seconds when she clocked 2:21:16 at London. Approximately how many years had the record stood?

A. 11 years; B. 13 years; C. 17 years; D. 22 years

109. At the 2004 Athens Olympic Marathon, Kastor finished in what place?

A. first; B; second; C. third; D. fourth

110. In the famous "Duel in the Sun" in the 1982 Boston Marathon, Alberto Salazar was pushed so hard by this man (just 2 seconds back!) that Salazar set what was then a course record of 2:08:52—and, according to some reports, received "Last Rites" after the race.

A. Jeff Wells; B. Dick Beardsley; C. Craig Virgin; D. John Lodwick

111. At the 1984 New York City Marathon, this Italian marathoner stopped eight times over the last few miles, but still held off a late charge from Englishman Dave Murphy, winning in a heat-slowed 2:14:58. (Hint: He won New York again in 1985, but never won an Olympic medal.)

A. Orlando Pizzolato; B. Gelindo Bordin; C. Alberto Cova; D. Gianni Poli

112. After winning the 1984 Chicago Marathon in a world record 2:08:05 (and defeating Olympic champ Carlos Lopes in the process), this affable Brit wit wryly noted: "I still have to get permission to go to a race at which I might win $10,000 or $15,000, far more than I earn in a full year with the R.A.F."

A. Nick Rose; B. Steve Jones; C. Charlie Spedding; D. Joe Strummer

113. In his first-ever marathon, this man placed second in the 1984 Olympic Games—a career highlight perhaps outdone only by his two World Cross-Country titles.

A. Karel Lismont of Belgium; B. John Treacy of Ireland; C. Charlie Spedding of Great Britain; D. Carlos Lopes of Portugal

114. This star of the Illinois AC was the U.S. national champion in the mile eight times, but his highest Olympic finish was a fifth in the marathon at Amsterdam in 1928, in addition to a third at the 1928 Boston Marathon.

A. Joie Ray; B. Ernie Banks; C. Chuck Mellor; D. John Daley

115. Forced to run for Japan (the occupiers of his country at the time) in the 1936 Olympic Games, this Korean runner—who also held the world record at the time—won the marathon by more than 2 minutes. In 1988, when Seoul hosted the Games, this same man proudly ran the Olympic torch into the stadium.

A. Kee Yong Hamm; B. Yun Bok Suh; C. Sohn Kee-chung; D. Lee Bong-Ju

116. Colleen De Reuck set a U.S. women's marathon trials record with her 2:28:25 at the 2004 race in St. Louis. She resides and trains in Boulder, Colorado, but prior to becoming a U.S. citizen, what country did she run for?

A. South Africa; B. Great Britain; C. Canada; D. The Netherlands

117. In the 1970s—the pioneer days of women's marathoning—this American twice held the world record and also won the 1973 Boston Marathon.

A. Kim Merritt; B. Gayle Barron; C. Patti Lyons; D. Jacqueline Hansen

118. Name the two Americans who won marathon medals at the 2004 Athens Olympic Games on a hot day and over a hilly course.

119. She won three consecutive Boston Marathons and in 1996 became the first African woman to win the Olympic Marathon.

A. Elana Meyer of South Africa; B. Fatuma Roba of Ethiopia; C. Catherine Ndereba of Kenya; D. Derartu Tulu of Ethiopia

120. This expat from South Africa won the 1993 World Championship Marathon gold while running for the U.S.A., his adopted country.

A. Mark Plaatjes; B. Johnny Halberstadt; C. Phillimon Hanneck; D. Darren De Reuck

121. Perhaps better known as a cross-country great, this man currently holds the world record for the men's marathon—a sizzling 2:04:55 at Berlin in 2003.

A. Paul Tergat of Kenya; B. Belayneh Dinsamo of Ethiopia; C. Cosmas Ndeti of Kenya; D. Khalid Khannouchi of the U.S.A.

122. How far back was second place in the above world record run?

A: 6 seconds; B. 1 minute, 6 seconds; C. 5 minutes; D. 1 second

123. En route to an American record and a Boston Marathon course record in 1975, hometown dark horse Bill Rodgers stopped:

A. twice to catch his breath; B. three times—once to tie his shoe, twice to drink water; C. four times to walk and massage sore quad muscles; D. once at 21 miles to kiss his wife at the top of Heartbreak Hill

124. At age 73, this man lowered his own age-group record for men in the 70-plus bracket to an incredible 2:54:49 at Toronto. Name him.

A. Ed Whitlock of Canada; B. Pierre Trudeau of Canada; C. Ken Sparks of the U.S.A.; D. Joop Ruter of the Netherlands

125. This man set the world record in the marathon twice—but for two different countries. Name him.

126. After his collapse from heatstroke in the 1954 Empire Games Marathon in Vancouver, hard-luck British standout Jim Peters was carried into the locker room and—still feverishly muddled— uttered these three words from his stretcher:

A. "Where am I?"; B. "Bring me beer!"; C. "God, glory, England!" D. "Did I win?"

127. This world-class marathoner (with wins at Boston, London, and Fukuoka) took a closer look at running after pitching for his youth baseball team and losing the game on a teammate's costly error.

A. Amby Burfoot; B. Bill Rodgers; C. Frank Shorter; D. Toshihiko Seko

MARATHON
ANSWERS

1. B
2. A
3. B
4. D
5. D
6. C
7. D
8. A
9. D
10. C
11. Francisco Lazaro
12. D
13. A
14. C
15. Khalid Khannouchi, U.S.A.; Paul Tergat, Kenya; Haile Gebrselassie, Ethiopia
16. D. Ceron, 1994-1996; Dorre, 1992-1994
17. A
18. A. Espinosa ran 2:08:46 at the 2003 Berlin Marathon.
19. D
20. A

21. C
22. A
23. D
24. D
25. D
26. D
27. C
28. C
29. B
30. B
31. A
32. A. Johnny Miles, after winning in 1926.
33. Brian Maxwell
34. A
35. B
36. C
37. C
38. A. Andersen-Scheiss finished 37th, though it took her 5 minutes, 44 seconds to complete her lap on the stadium track.
39. D
40. He ran barefoot and broke the world record by less than a second.
41. Depressed because of what he believed to be a career-ending injury, he committed suicide.
42. D
43. B
44. D
45. D
46. B
47. C

48. B
49. B
50. B
51. B
52. Joan Benoit Samuelson of the U.S.A., Rosa Mota of Portugal, Fatuma Roba of Ethiopia
53. A
54. Kathrine Switzer
55. Jock Semple
56. B
57. D
58. C
59. D
60. C
61. B
62. D
63. B
64. C
65. D
66. C
67. C
68. C
69. D
70. C
71. A
72. A
73. B
74. A
75. C
76. D

77. C

78. C

79. B

80. C

81. D

82. B

83. B

84. C

85. D

86. A

87. C

88. B

89. A

90. A

91. D

92. A

93. A

94. B

95. B

96. A

97. C

98. D (John A. Kelley had seven second-place finishes at Boston; John J. Kelley had five.)

99. D

100. C

101. "No, Emil, the pace it is too slow."

102. A

103. New Zealand, with three bronze. Australia has one silver.

104. A

105. B

106. A

107. C

108. C

109. C

110. B

111. A

112. B

113. B

114. A

115. C

116. A

117. D

118. Meb Keflezighi and Deena Drossin Kastor

119. B

120. A

121. A

122. Sammy Korir of Kenya was officially timed in 2:04:56 . . . just one tick back!

123. B

124. A

125. Khalid Khannouchi for both Morocco and the U.S.A.

126. D

127. D

COACHES

There were more than a few great runners who never wanted, or even consulted, a coach. One of the most interesting cases of an athlete-coach relationship involves Roger Bannister and the Austrian-born coach Franz Stampfl. Stampfl trained Bannister's pacemakers for the four-minute-mile assault, but Bannister himself tended to resist what he viewed as any inordinate dependence on a coach. In fact, prior to meeting Stampfl in the fall of 1953, Bannister said he was "something of a loner without a coach."

And although Bannister sometimes seems to dance around any defining statement—such as "Franz Stampfl was my coach"—he readily acknowledges that Stampfl's planning proved to be an important contribution to attacking the 4-minute-mile barrier. Perhaps even more crucial was Stampfl's work with Chris Chataway and Chris Brasher; his workouts put that pair in peak shape and that allowed them to pace Bannister through three-quarters of that famous mile. Nevertheless, the transition—from self-coached to assistance from Stampfl—was not an easy one for Bannister, even with the pressure of "the big race" on the immediate horizon.

"I would have liked [Stampfl's] advice and help at this moment, but I could not bring myself to ask him. It was as if now, at the end of my running career, I was being forced to admit that coaches were necessary after all," said Bannister (in his best-selling autobiography *The Four Minute Mile*), referring to the days leading up to his world-record mile on May 6, 1954.

Stampfl, in an interview with the ever-dogged Australian running journalist Brian Lenton (*Through the Tape*), also said this: "When he arrived at Iffley Road track . . . Roger was in a blue mood . . . Chataway and Brasher had to persuade him to run. I knew a bit of rain and wind would make no bloody difference because [Bannister] was capable of a 3:56 or 3:57 mile."

There seem to be two schools on this subject of coaches. One is that the runner should not worry about the day-to-day planning—the workouts, what races to run—that's the coach's job. "Act like a horse. Be dumb. Just run," quipped Jim "Jumbo" Elliott, the highly successful Villanova coach.

Two, be your own man. Rise to the heights of Mount Olympus, or go down like a shooting star—but make your own decisions. In the words of Jack Foster, the successful, self-directed marathoner (particularly as a master) from New Zealand: "Coaches are okay, I guess, but I prefer to do things my own way."

Paavo Nurmi, flinty and self-reliant, was not all that enamored with coaches, either. In fact, he was miffed that the Finnish national team officials prevented him from running the 10,000 meters at the 1924 Paris Olympic Games. They claimed he was entering too many events for his own good.

Years later, it was said that Lasse Viren's coach approached the long-retired Nurmi for some tips on how to dispense advice to runners. A man of few words and none of those sugar coated, Nurmi replied: "If you want to say something to an athlete, say it quickly and give no alternatives. This is a game of winning and losing. It is senseless to explain and explain."

Having been both a coach and an athlete, I would have to say that being a coach is more nerve-racking. As a runner, you are able to disperse your nervous energy in the competition—but as a coach, I often found myself sleepless prior to important meets, and nearly sleepless afterward. Furthermore, when one of my worthy runners was injured, I felt almost equally afflicted—in some cases, more than willing to change places with the luckless athlete had something like that actually been possible. In my experience, that's the hardest part of coaching; the other stuff is no big deal.

There is a story that one of Mihaly Igloi's great runners once arrived at the track to train. The dawn broke with reluctance, dismal and drizzly. Perhaps no one would be there? When the runner peered bleary-eyed into the stadium he spied Igloi—the famed Hungarian coach—already there, waiting patiently for his charges to arrive.

1. His "Spartan" training camp at Portsea was infamous—particularly for repeat hill runs up the towering Australian sand dunes, including one aptly dubbed "Agony."

A. Steve Moneghetti; B. Franz Stampfl; C. Percy Cerutty; D. Pat Clohessy

2. This coach crossed a moat and began wildly waving a towel to encourage his ace middle-distance runner on the gun lap at the Olympic Games in Rome. The Italian police corralled the coach, and he was lucky to avoid a night in the slammer for his display of unbridled enthusiasm. Name this eccentric coach.

3. **GOLD-MEDAL QUESTION.** This German coach is generally regarded as the first to employ "interval training" in the 1930s.

4. The jury is still out on whether or not this man "coached" Roger Bannister (who wasn't all that keen on coaches) prior to the attempt to break the 4-minute mile. Certainly he offered the young Englishman some "advice" and absolutely got Bannister's pacesetters ready to rock. Who was he?

A. Sam Mussabini; B. Harry Wilson; C. Peter Coe; D. Franz Stampfl

5. As one of the "pioneers" at Nike, this coach allegedly wrecked his wife's waffle iron while attempting to make waffle-soled running shoes.

6. How did Coach Jim "Jumbo" Elliott get his nickname?

A. He worked at the Philadelphia zoo, cleaning elephant cages; B. A baseball pitcher for a Philadelphia team named Jim Elliott was nicknamed "Jumbo"; C. He always opted for jumbo-sized sodas on the golf course; D. Before he became a runner, he played midget football and was the biggest kid on his team

7. There's a statue of Jumbo Elliott at the Villanova track depicting the great coach holding what in his hand?

A. a stopwatch; B. a baton; C. a Celtic cross; D. a clipboard

8. **BRONZE-MEDAL QUESTION.** A former All-American steeplechase runner for Villanova, this coach's Haverford College men's distance runners are always among the best in NCAA Division III circles—or even in open competition. He also coached Sydney Maree in that great runner's postcollegiate days.

9. A famous Hungarian coach and some of his best runners did what after the 1956 Melbourne Olympic Games in Australia?

10. Name that famous Hungarian coach. In addition to his great Hungarian runners, he also coached some top Americans.

11. True or False. A coach from the Atlantic Coast Conference climbed a bell tower on campus and used binoculars to observe the Hungarian coach's methods as he trained his runners.

12. In the film *Chariots of Fire* this man who coached Harold Abrahams of Great Britain says (in regard to speed): "In our business, son, we have a saying: 'You can't put in what God left out!'"

A. Sam Mussabini; B. Bill Pearson; C. Percy Cerutty; D. Sam Dee

13. "Everybody and their mother knows you don't train hard on Friday if you're racing on Saturday," this highly successful Villanova coach once stated. "But Thursday is the most dangerous day of the week." (Hint: He guided his team to a slew of consecutive NCAA Division I cross-country titles.)

14. Although he conferred with Coach Bill Bowerman, the man who worked most directly with Steve Prefontaine was this long-distance Olympic medal winner who later coached at Oregon. Name him.

A. Jim Ryun; B. Bob Schul; C. Billy Mills; D. Bill Dellinger

15. If you add all this coach's NCAA Division I men's titles together—including cross-country, indoor track, and outdoor track—he's definitely got more than just "luck of the Irish" working for him. Name him and his university.

16. This coach really put a tiger in the tank of this women's track-and-field program, with NCAA Division I outdoor championship wins in double figures.

17. True or False. The program referred to in the previous question has more team NCAA D-I women's outdoor track titles—13— than all the other teams combined, as of 2005.

18. This Japanese coach preached discipline and *Zensoho* ("running with Zen") to his charges. Name him.

19. In his book *Sub-4:00: Alan Webb and the Quest for the Fastest Mile,* what coach is Chris Lear writing about in Chapter Four, titled "The War Dog"?

20. In Lear's book *Running with the Buffaloes* this coach is at the helm through a thrilling but sometimes tumultuous cross-country season. Name him.

21. This Canadian coach co-authored *Speed Trap: Inside the Biggest Scandal in Olympic History* after his top sprinter tested his positive in 1988. Name the coach.

22. This coach (highly successful at Wisconsin years ago) recently left Oregon and will be the new head coach at Oklahoma.

23. This coach, successful at Dartmouth and highly successful at Stanford, was named the new coach at Oregon in 2005. Name him.

24. He's best known for instructing Kiwis, but this famous coach also offered his knowledge in foreign countries, such as Finland, Denmark, Mexico, and Venezuela. Name the man and his home country.

25. Not only does this man coach at Shippensburg University in Pennsylvania, but he once won a bronze medal in the World Championship Marathon. A former U.S. Olympian, he's now one of the top masters in the world.

26. He's the last American runner to snag an Olympic medal in the steeplechase. He's now a highly successful coach at Division III powerhouse Calvin College in Michigan.

A. George Young; B. Henry Marsh; C. Marc Davis; D. Brian Diemer

27. This man has contributed to the sport of running in many different ways—coaching, writing, and research in exercise physiology. His women's teams at Cortland State in New York won numerous NCAA Division III titles in cross-country. Name him.

28. Name four former world-class milers who are now head coaches on the U.S. college scene. Hint: The *slow* guys in this bunch ran 3:51 for the mile.

29. If someone asked you if Joe Paterno or this guy has been coaching at Penn State the longest, you'd have to think about it. Name this veteran PSU cross-country/track coach.

30. He coached more than 100 All-Americans, most of them sprinters. No wonder San Jose was nicknamed "Speed City" while he coached at San Jose State. Name him.

31. Nicknamed the "Maker of Champions," this coach guided the USC Trojans to 12 NCAA titles—including 9 straight—in track and field. (Hint: Despite all that conquering, his first name wasn't Oliver.) Name him.

A: John McKay; B. Brutus Hamilton; C. Dean Cromwell; D. Paul Westphal

32. "The athletes have to give up a little freedom, and the country needs to give up two or three MX missiles," this man quipped, concerning what it takes to have a successful Olympic team. He coached at Stanford and served as an Olympic coach in 1984.

A. Jumbo Elliott; B. Brooks Johnson; C. Mel Rosen; D. Dean Cromwell

33. SILVER-MEDAL QUESTION. This coach won the Comrades Marathon five times during his career in the 1920s, plus set world records for 50 and 100 miles in his day. He's regarded as the patron saint of long-distance running in South Africa. Name him.

34. The onslaught of Chinese women distance runners in the mid-1990s sent shock waves of controversy and suspicion through the world of track and field. Who coached these record-smashers?

35. True or False. The same coach in the previous question once said this about his runners: "I would scold them or beat them when they were lazy or disobedient. But I only did it for their own good."

36. Because there weren't funds for coaches not part of the official team, Coach Bob Granger reportedly worked his way over on a freighter to see this star sprinter—an Olympic gold-medal winner in both the 100- and 200-meter races—defeat the world's fastest in Amsterdam. Who was the great sprinter Granger coached?

A. Percy Williams of Canada; B. Jackson Scholz of the U.S.A.; C. Charley Paddock of the U.S.A.; D. Eddie Tolan of the U.S.A.

37. This coach—more than three decades at high-altitude Adams State in Colorado—said: "I'm in heaven here . . . And my runners are my angels."

MATCH THE ATHLETE WITH THE COACH

Part 1

1. Lynn Jennings	A. Percy Cerutty
2. Alan Webb	B. Waldemer Gerschler
3. Bob Schul	C. Tom Tellez
4. Herb Elliott	D. Johan Kaggestad
5. Abebe Bikila	E. Harry Groves
6. Ralph Doubell	F. Rolf Haikkola
7. Steve Scott	G. Dean Cromwell
8. Lasse Viren	H. Bob Sevene
9. Steve Ovett	I. Scott Raczko
10. Grete Waitz	J. Onni Niskanen
11. Rudolph Harbig	K. Mihaly Igloi
12. Joan Benoit Samuelson	L. Pat Clohessy
13. Charley Paddock	M. John Babington
14. Carl Lewis	N. Doug Brown
15. Rob de Castella	O. Bob Larsen
16. Marty Liquori	P. Marshall Clark
17. Todd Williams	Q. Harry Wilson
18. Meb Keflezighi	R. Franz Stampfl
19. Greg Fredericks	S. Jumbo Elliott
20. Don Kardong	T. Len Miller

MATCH THE ATHLETE WITH THE COACH

Part 2

1. Albie Thomas	A. Fred Wilt
2. Merv Lincoln	B. Dieter Hogan
3. Buddy Edelen	C. Peter Tegen
4. Bob Kennedy	D. Joe Vigil
5. Peter Snell	E. Bob Giegengack
6. Deena Drossin Kastor	F. Kiyoshi Nakamura
7. Jim Beatty	G. Bob Timmons
8. Jim Ryun	H. Arthur Lydiard
9. Alberto Salazar	I. Bill Bowerman
10. John Walker	J. Percy Cerutty
11. Douglas Wakiihuri	K. Bill Dellinger
12. Kenny Moore	L. Ron Warhurst
13. Dave Wottle	M. Arch Jelley
14. Amy Rudolf	N. Mark Wetmore
15. Kevin Sullivan	O. Clyde Hart
16. Suzy Favor Hamilton	P. Sam Bell
17. Michael Johnson	Q. Franz Stampfl
18. Adam Goucher	R. Mel Brodt
19. Frank Shorter	S. Mihlay Igloi
20. Uta Pippig	T. Ray Treacy

COACHES
ANSWERS

1. C
2. Percy Cerutty
3. Waldemar Gerschler
4. D
5. Bill Bowerman
6. B
7. A
8. Tom Donnelley
9. They all defected to the West. Hungary was under Communist rule at that time.
10. Mihaly Igloi
11. True, at least according to Oregon's Bill Bowerman. Bowerman said Dale Ranson of North Carolina secretly watched Igloi conduct his track sessions, then "borrowed" some the same ideas.
12. A
13. Marty Stern
14. D
15. John McDonnell of Arkansas
16. Pat Henry of LSU
17. True. As of 2005, LSU 13, everyone else 11.
18. Kiyoshi Nakamura
19. Ron Warhurst, head coach at Michigan

20. Mark Wetmore
21. Charlie Francis
22. Martin Smith
23. Vin Lalanna
24. Arthur Lydiard of New Zealand
25. Steve Spence
26. D
27. Jack Daniels
28. Marcus O'Sullivan at Villanova; Steve Scott at Cal State San Marcos; Jim Spivey at Vanderbilt; John Gregorek at Brown
29. Harry Groves
30. Lloyd "Bud" Winter
31. C
32. B
33. Arthur Newton
34. Ma Junren
35. True! Do you still think your high school coach was mean?
36. A
37. Joe Vigil

Match the athlete with the coach, Part 1
1. M 2. I 3. K 4. A 5. J 6. R 7. T 8. F 9. Q 10. D 11. B
12. H 13. G 14. C 15. L 16. S 17. N 18. O 19. E 20. P

Match the athlete with the coach, Part 2
1. J 2. Q 3. A 4. P 5. H 6. D 7. S 8. G 9. K 10. M 11. F
12. I 13. R 14. T 15. L 16. C 17. O 18. N 19. E 20. B

MY OLD SCHOOL

(Match the runner to the college or university)

MY OLD SCHOOL 1

1. **Abdi Bile** (Somalia, 1987 1500-meter world champ; 2-time NCAA outdoor 1500-meter winner)

2. **Suleiman Nyambui** (Tanzania, multi-time NCAA champ; 1980 Olympic silver medal in the 5000 meters)

3. **Archie San Romani** (1935 outdoor NCAA mile champ, 4th in the 1936 Olympic 1500)

4. **Ron Delany** (Ireland, 1956 Olympic champ for 1500 meters; 2-time NCAA outdoor mile champ)

5. **Kenny Moore** (4th in 1972 Olympic Marathon, national cross-country champ in 1967)

6. **Nick Rose** (Great Britain, NCAA cross-country champ; 3rd in World Cross-Country, 1979)

7. **John Treacy** (Ireland, 2-time World Cross-Country champ; Olympic silver in the marathon)

8. **Louis Zamperini** (2-time NCAA outdoor mile champ in the 1930s; Berlin Olympic 5000 final)

9. **Frank Shorter** (1972 Olympic Marathon champ, 2nd in 1976

10. **Bill Rodgers** (4-time Boston Marathon winner)

11. **Bob Kennedy** (2-time NCAA cross-country champ; Olympian)

12. **Ed Eyestone** (2-time NCAA 10,000-meter champ; Olympian)

13. **Noureddine Morceli** (Algeria, Olympic 1500 champ, former world-record holder in the mile)

A. VILLANOVA
B. PROVIDENCE
C. OREGON
D. WESLEYAN
E. WESTERN KENTUCKY
F. EMPORIA STATE
G. RIVERSIDE CC
H. GEORGE MASON
I. INDIANA
J. BRIGHAM YOUNG
K. YALE
L. SOUTHERN CAL
M. TEXAS-EL PASO

MY OLD SCHOOL 2

1. **Edwin Moses** (3-time Olympic medalist, 400m-hurdle great)

2. **Don Kardong** (U.S. Olympic marathon, *Runner's World* writer)

3. **Dick Buerkle** (2-time Olympian, world-class marks in mile and 5000)

4. **Billy Mills** (Olympic great, world-record setter)

5. **Mary Decker Slaney** (set numerous world and U.S. records)

6. **Lynn Jennings** (multi-time cross-country champ, Worlds and U.S. Olympic medal)

7. **Pete Pfitzinger** (2-time Olympic marathon man, *Running Times* columnist)

8. **Tim Broe** (NCAA steeple champ, cross-country standout, Olympic 5000 runner)

9. **Carl Lewis** (King Carl! Need we say more?)

10. **Madeline Manning** (numerous Olympic teams, Olympic gold)

11. **Horace Ashenfelter** (1952 Olympic champ, world-record holder)

12. Pat Porter (multi-time U.S. cross-country champ)

13. Ray Barbuti (1928 400-meter champ, college football captain)

A. PRINCETON
B. COLORADO
C. ALABAMA
D. CORNELL
E. TENNESSEE STATE
F. STANFORD
G. MOORHOUSE
H. PENN STATE
I. HOUSTON
J. KANSAS
K. SYRACUSE
L. VILLANOVA
M. ADAMS STATE

MY OLD SCHOOL 3

1. **Elizabeth Robinson** (Olympic sprint star)

2. **Sonia O'Sullivan** (Ireland, world-class distance runner)

3. **Craig Virgin** (cross-country great; former 10,000-meter standout)

4. **Liz Lynch McColgan** (Scotland, NYC Marathon winner; Olympic medalist)

5. **Dave Wottle** (NCAA champ; Olympic kick king)

6. **Dan Browne** (2004 Olympic marathoner)

7. **Frank O'Mara** (Ireland, sub-4 miler; NCAA 1500 champ)

8. **Renaldo Nehemiah** (hurdler extraordinaire)

9. **Joachim Cruz** (Brazil, multi-time NCAA champ; Olympic standout)

10. **Bill Bonthron** (former world-record holder in several middle-distance events; NCAA champ)

11. **Harrison Dillard** (Olympic star, multi-time NCAA champ)

A. OREGON
B. WEST POINT
C. ARKANSAS
D. MARYLAND
E. BALDWIN-WALLACE
F. NORTHWESTERN
G. ILLINOIS
H. ALABAMA
I. VILLANOVA
J. BOWLING GREEN
K. PRINCETON

MY OLD SCHOOL 4

1. **Vic Zowlak** (2-time NCAA steeplechase champ; Olympian)

2. **Danny Harris** (Olympic medal winner; multi-time NCAA champ)

3. **David Hemery** (Great Britain, NCAA champ; Olympic medalist)

4. **Arturo Barrios** (Mexico, world-record-setting distance runner)

5. **Angela Chalmers** (Canada, NCAA cross-country champ; Olympic bronze-medal winner)

6. **Bobby Joe Morrow** (1950s sprint star in NCAA and Olympic competition)

7. **Merlene Ottey** (Jamaica, NCAA champ; Olympic sprint star)

8. **Ralph Metcalfe** (multi-time NCAA champ; Olympic sprint star)

9. **Amby Burfoot** (Boston Marathon winner; *Runner's World* editor, writer)

10. **Lasse Viren** (Olympic great; very brief stay on U.S. college scene)

11. **Bruce Jenner** (1976 Olympic decathlon champ)

12. **Bob Schul** (1964 Olympic champ)

13. **Jim Grelle** (Ryun rival, former U.S. mile record holder)

A. ABILENE CHRISTIAN
B. MIAMI OF OHIO
C. WESLEYAN
D. GRACELAND COLLEGE
E. BOSTON COLLEGE
F. TEXAS A&M
G. NORTHERN ARIZONA
H. NEBRASKA
I. BRIGHAM YOUNG
J. OREGON
K. VILLANOVA
L. MARQUETTE
M. IOWA STATE

MY OLD SCHOOL 5

1. **Jon Sinclair** (road race standout; U.S. cross-country champion)

2. **Michael Johnson** (Olympic sprint great)

3. **Craig Masback** (USA Track CEO; former world-class miler)

4. **Herb McKenley** (Jamaican Olympic star sprinter)

5. **Justin Gatlin** (NCAA, world, and Olympic sprint champ)

6. **Shalane Flanagan** (middle- and long-distance standout; NCAA champ)

7. **Alan Webb** (Mr. Mile in America; short college stay)

8. **Joan Benoit Samuelson** (marathon star; missed her native Maine at this school)

9. **Paul Ereng** (Kenya, 2-lap whiz kid)

10. **Andrew Rock** (4 x 400 Olympic gold; world 400 silver)

11. **Don Lash** (cross-country king of his era)

12. **Bob Kempainen** (former U.S. marathon record)

13. **Florence Griffith Joyner** ('88 Olympic sprint sensation; late great "Flo Jo")

A. UCLA
B. DARTMOUTH
C. TENNESSEE
D. COLORADO STATE
E. NORTH CAROLINA STATE
F. ILLINOIS
G. WISCONSIN-OSHKOSH
H. INDIANA
I. MICHIGAN
J. BAYLOR
K. NORTH CAROLINA
L. VIRGINIA
M. PRINCETON

MY OLD SCHOOL 6

1. **Marla Runyan** (world-class times from the 1500 to the marathon)

2. **Rick Wohlhutter** (Olympic medal winner; held world and U.S. records)

3. **David Krummernacker** (800 hotshot; indoor world and NCAA champ)

4. **Meb Keflezighi** (Olympic marathon medalist; top-notch 10-K man)

5. **Brian Sell** (led 2004 U.S. Marathon Trials for 20-plus miles; 9th at Worlds)

6. **Mary Jane Harrelson** (2-time NCAA 1500 champ)

7. **Deena Drossin Kastor** (Olympic Marathon medal; always tough at World Cross-Country)

8. **Eammon Coghlan** (Ireland, indoor mile king; Olympic just-misses)

9. **Sid Sink** (2-time NCAA steeplechase champ)

10. **Barney Ewell** (won 4 NCAA sprint titles; Olympic medal winner)

11. **Amy Rudolf** (2-time Olympic distance runner; former NCAA champ in 1500 meters)

12. **Dave Sime** (NCAA sprint star; Olympic runner-up in 1960)

13. **Clarence DeMar** (multi-time Boston Marathon winner; ran college cross-country)

A. VILLANOVA
B. DUKE
C. PENN STATE
D. MESSIAH/ST. FRANCIS
E. SAN DIEGO STATE
F. VERMONT
G. NOTRE DAME
H. GEORGIA TECH
I. PROVIDENCE
J. APPALACIAN STATE
K. ARKANSAS
L. BOWLING GREEN
M. UCLA

MY OLD SCHOOL 7

1. **Herb Lindsey** (top gun on U.S. roads in the early 1980s)

2. **Byron Dyce** (Jamaica, NCAA 800-champ; sub-4 miler

3. **Carole Zajac** (2-time NCAA cross-country champ, former NCAA 10,000 record holder)

4. **Jim Svenoy** (Norway, 2-time NCAA steeplechase champ; Olympian)

5. **Garry Bjorklund** (U.S. Olympian for 10,000 meters)

6. **Regina Jacobs** (U.S. Olympian, multi-time 1500-meter champ)

7. **Glenn Hardin** (Olympic hurdle champ, multi-time NCAA champion)

8. **Gwyn Hardesty Coogan** (U.S. Olympian, 1991 U.S. cross-country runner-up)

9. **John Gregorek** (steeplechase star, sub-4 miler)

10. **Dyrol Burleson** (Olympian; once set U.S. mile record)

11. **Paul Cummings** (3:56 mile and a solid marathon)

12. **Francie Larrieu-Smith** (U.S. Olympian, 5th in '88 Olympic 10,000; 2-time U.S. cross-country champ)

A. LONG BEACH STATE
B. STANFORD
C. MINNESOTA
D. TEXAS-EL PASO
E. SMITH COLLEGE
F. NEW YORK UNIVERSITY
G. BRIGHAM YOUNG
H. OREGON
I. LOUSIANNA STATE
J. VILLANOVA
K. MICHIGAN STATE
L. GEORGETOWN

MY OLD SCHOOL 8

1. **Archie Hahn** (The "Milwaukee Meteor," but he ran college track in another state)

2. **Allan Lawrence** (Australia, 2-time NCAA 3-mile champ; Olympic bronze)

3. **George Rhoden** (Jamaica, Olympic medal winner; NCAA champ)

4. **Suzy Favor Hamilton** (multi-time NCAA champ; Olympian)

5. **Tommie Smith** (Olympic gold; world-record sprinter)

6. **Vicki Huber** (NCAA cross-country and multi-time track champ; Olympian)

7. **Lynn Williams** (Canada, plucky runner; Olympic bronze in '84 3000 mash-up)

8. **Tom Courtney** (Olympic and NCAA glory)

9. **Melody Fairchild** (Foot Locker champ; won NCAA 3000 indoor title in 1996)

10. **Phil Edwards** (Canada, 400-800 great; Olympic man of bronze)

11. **Curtis Mills** (first guy to break 45 seconds in NCAA 440 championship race)

12. **Ralph Mann** (3-time NCAA 440-yard hurdle champ; Olympic medal)

A. SAN DIEGO STATE
B. TEXAS A&M
C. FORDHAM
D. OREGON
E. HOUSTON
F. MICHIGAN
G. WISCONSIN
H. NEW YORK UNIVERSITY
I. BRIGHAM YOUNG
J. VILLANOVA
K. SAN JOSE STATE
L. MORGAN STATE

MY OLD SCHOOL
ANSWERS

Part 1 1. H 2. M 3. F 4. A 5. C 6. E 7. B 8. L 9. K 10. D
11. I 12. J 13. G

Part 2 1. G 2. F 3. L 4. J 5. B 6. A 7. D 8. C 9. I 10. E 11. H
12. M 13. K

Part 3 1. F 2. I 3. G 4. H 5. J 6. B 7. C 8. D 9. A 10. K
11. E

Part 4 1. K 2. M 3. E 4. F 5. G 6. A 7. H 8. L 9. C 10. I
11. D 12. B 13. J

Part 5 1. D 2. J 3. M 4. F 5. C 6. K 7. I 8. E 9. L 10. G
11. H 12. B 13. A

Part 6 1. E 2. G 3. H 4. M 5. D 6. J 7. K 8. A 9. L 10. C
11. I 12. B 13. F

Part 7 1. K 2. F 3. J 4. D 5. C 6. B 7. I 8. E 9. L 10. H
11. G 12. A

Part 8 1. F 2. E 3. L 4. G 5. K 6. J 7. A 8. C 9. D 10. H
11. B 12. I

RACES

The Berwick "Run for the Diamonds" race—one of the oldest in the country, dating back to 1908—has always drawn a lot of Canadian runners to take on its rugged route, which includes a two-mile uphill section between the two and four-mile mark. The boys from The Great White North have been making the trek down to Pennsylvania for decades, to participate in this challenging 9-mile Thanksgiving Day event.

The Canadian King of these trips down from Ontario had to be Wilmer "Whitey" Sheridan of the Hamilton Olympic Club. Sheridan, who completed his 50th Berwick race back in 1997 at age 80, once related one of my favorite running stories—a story beautiful in its simplicity.

Whitey was talking about what great lengths the Canadian runners went to just to race, particularly during the early 1940s, when gasoline and rubber were difficult to come by because of World War II rationing. "What we used to do, before we'd come down to Berwick," said Whitey, "is get what cars we had together. Then we'd pick the tires with most tread. We'd take one of one car, another off another...And, after we got four decent ones, we were ready to go."

Imagine that! A bunch of young Canadian guys, taking tires of off cars—putting them on one vehicle—simply so it would be safe enough to drive hundreds of miles to a race. The trip itself took some time, too, since this was all pre-superhighways. Nevertheless, those Canadians always seemed to find a way. They loved competitive running that much.

The Canadians didn't always arrive empty handed, either. There's a story that several of them—including Canadian Olympian Scotty Rankin—once brought a bunch of frozen steaks down to Johnny Kelley when they arrived to run the Boston Marathon. No doubt the steaks were merrily accepted, since meat was rationed during the war years.

It really wasn't until the 1970s that road racing began to blossom around the United States. Until that time, it usually took a bit of traveling to find a race. It wasn't as if you could race every weekend; you had to search for them. There were dozens of races around the country; but not hundreds and hundreds of them.

In this day of jet-age travel, we also tend to forget what it was like for the runners of yesteryear to travel across the ocean to compete. For example, in 1936, the U.S. Olympic team left New York City on the *Manhattan* and it took a week before they reached Hamburg, Germany. The athletes were limited to how much training they could do on deck, but apparently there was more than enough food to go around. Then only 19 years old, Louis Zamperini—a member of the American 5000-meter contingent—claimed he gained too much weight on the journey across the Atlantic because he was stuffing down food like a shot putter!

With Frank Shorter's gold medal win in the Munich Olympic Marathon, road races were soon popping up like dandelions in your backyard. Many of the biggest road races in the United States were created soon after the 1972 Games and Shorter's great triumph landed him on the front cover of *Life* magazine. Now it's rarely a problem of where to find a race, simply a decision of which one to choose. If you're looking for more help in that department, check out the State Race trivia section!

1. It's the oldest road race in North America.

A. The Around the Bay 30-K, Hamilton, Ontario; B. Boston Marathon; C. Yonkers Marathon, Yonkers, New York; D. The Dipsea Race

2. This race was co-sponsored by a local newspaper and a:

A. gambling house; B. bar; C. cigar store; D. dog racing track

3. The first edition of North America's oldest road race went to the starting line on:

A. April 1—April Fools' Day; B. Patriots' Day; C. Christmas Day; D. the Fourth of July

4. His total of seven victories is the record for that oldest race.

A. Scotty Rankine; B. Peter Maher; C. Gerard Cote; D. Jerome Drayton

5. The first *ekiden* relay (*eki* means "station" in Japanese, and *den* means "to transmit") in Japan was held in 1917. The races are very popular in Japan. What do relay runners pass instead a baton?

6. BRONZE-MEDAL QUESTION. What is the Japanese word for this item passed between runners?

7. The first road race exclusively for women was this 10-K race in Central Park, conducted by the New York Road Runners Club in 1972.

8. Only 78 runners competed in that inaugural event, though the field has been more than 6,000 over the years. But who won the first race, in a now modest time of 37:01?

A. Nina Kuscsik; B. Joan Benoit Samuelson; C. Kathrine Switzer; D. Jackie Dixon

9. True or False. No woman has ever broken 31 minutes (5-minute-per-mile race pace) for the challenging Central Park course of rolling hills.

10. Two women have won this race a record five times—one from Norway and one from Kenya. Name them.

11. In a barroom, it's sometimes slang for a beer and whiskey mixed together. But in Utica, New York, it means 15K racing at its best. You can also visit the National Distance Running Hall of

Fame in town. Name the race.

12. True or False. Atlanta's Peachtree Road Race 10-K went from 110 runners in 1970 to more than 20,000 in 10 years.

13. The first winners of the Peachtree Road Race were a guy who made the 1972 Olympic team (also a running writer/coach) and a local woman who went on to win the 1978 Boston Marathon.

14. Many world-class runners have taken on a hill called *Ahogillo* ("Out of Breath") at the San Blas Half-Marathon. The race dates back to 1957. Where is it held?

A. Kingston, Jamaica; B. Rio de Janeiro, Brazil; C. Coamo, Puerto Rico; D. Mexico City, Mexico

15. **SILVER-MEDAL QUESTION.** Later a college coach, this native New York Athletic Club runner twice won the rugged San Blas race (1967, 1968). He was the only American to accomplish this feat, until Khalid Khannouchi (after a change of citizenship) won it in 2002.

16. From 1974 through 1978, these two marathon greats won five straight Falmouth Road Race titles between themselves—arguably the heyday of American distance running. Name them.

17. This Kenyan runner shattered the Falmouth Road Race record in 2004, clocking 31:08 for the 7-mile route. Name him.

A. Gilbert Okari; B. Paul Tergat; C. Henry Rono; D. Moses Kiptanui

18. This famous runner leads the all-time pack with six career victories at Falmouth. Name this great racer.

A. Lornah Kiplagat of Kenya; B. Bill Rodgers of the U.S.A.; C. Joan Benoit Samuelson of the U.S.A.; D. Rod Dixon of New Zealand

19. You know you're near the 1-mile mark at Falmouth when you see this famous landmark.

A. The Prudential Tower; B. The Nobska Lighthouse; C. Captain Kidd's grave; D. The Woods Hole drawbridge

20. A "bandit" or a "crasher" is someone who does what at a road race?

21. This man's five titles comprise a Quad City Times Bix-7 record on that hilly course.

A. Gilbert Okari of Kenya; B. Bill Rodgers of the U.S.A.; C. Mark Curp of the U.S.A.; D. John Korir of Kenya

22. Lilac Bloomsday got its name—via Irish writer James Joyce—from this founding "father" and former U.S. Olympian. He placed third in the inaugural event, won by Frank Shorter.

23. This runner from New Zealand has amassed more titles—an astounding seven—at this Spokane-based race, more than any other racer in its more than 30-year history.

A. Anne Audain; B. Lorraine Moller; C. Dick Quax; D. Rod Dixon

24. **GOLD MEDAL QUESTION.** Now called "Bay to Breakers," this popular 12-K run in San Francisco dates back to 1912. It was originally called what?

25. The first race in 1912 was organized with what purpose in mind?

A. to promote overall fitness; B. to bolster morale as the city continued to rebuild after its devastating earthquake of 1906; C. to give gamblers something to bet on before horse racing season began; D. to begin training American runners for the next Olympic Marathon

26. Although this will seem strangely unlikely to anyone who has ever tried to run Bay to Breakers, the 1963 event drew a pathetic 25 entries. At its highest, however, Bay to Breakers has been estimated at how many participants?

A. 35,000-plus; B. 50,000-plus, C. 90,000-plus; D. more than 100,000

27. A race within the race involves teams of runners dressed up as these creepy crawlers.

A. ants; B. spiders; C. centipedes; D. mice

28. True or False. It's not at all unusual to see runners au naturel or dressed like Elvis in this crazy event.

29. True or False. Some runners called "spawning salmon" go against the tide—starting at the finish line and finishing at the starting line.

30. The City to Surf 12-K in Sydney, Australia, came about after this happened.

A. Frank Shorter's Olympic Marathon win was broadcast around the world; B. a newspaper clipping about Bay to Breakers was sent to a newspaper in Sydney; C. Derek Clayton the world record in the marathon; D. Herb Elliott won Olympic gold in Rome

31. True or False. No man has ever broken 40 minutes for 12-K in the City to Surf race as of 2005.

32. In 1987 Australian Brad Camp (40:15) scored a 1-second win over this sturdy-looking American road racer, in City to Surf's closest race ever. Name the Yank.

A. Kenny Moore; B. Bill Rodgers; C. Mark Curp; D. Herb Lindsay

33. Although Australians have dominated their own event, one of the *wrong* answers from the previous question won the first City to Surf race in 1971. Who?

34. Until Susie Power blasted 45:08 in 2001, this famous Australian runner—an Olympic medal winner—had the course record for women at 45:47. It lasted 13 years. Name her.

35. Four times under 28 minutes for 10-K on the roads attest to this man's abilities at that distance, including a U.S. record of 27:22.6 at the Crescent City Classic in New Orleans in 1984. Who was he?

A. Alberto Salazar; B. Bob Kennedy; C. Mark Nenow; D. Todd Williams

36. This world-class runner—on roads, track, or cross-country—has broken an hour for the half-marathon on at least seven occasions.

A. Antonio Pinto of Portugal; B. Haile Gebrselassie of Ethiopia; C. Moses Tanui of Kenya; D. Paul Tergat of Kenya

37. According to the International Association of Athletics Federation (IAAF), her 1:08:34 for the 1984 Philadelphia Distance Run is still the fastest half-marathon run in North America on a certified course.

A. Grete Waitz of Norway; B. Joan Benoit Samuelson of the U.S.A.; C. Liz Lynch McColgan of Great Britain; D. Rosa Mota of Portugal

38. Although she announced her retirement in 2005, this African runner set half-marathon (1:06:44) and 15-K (46:57) records. She also snagged a silver medal in the 1992 Olympic 10,000.

A. Elana Meyer of South Africa; B. Zola Budd of South Africa; C. Tegla Laroupe of Kenya; D. Derartu Tulu of Ethiopia

39. She's run 1:05:40 on the Great North Half-Marathon course in Newcastle, England, but its slightly downhill route doesn't allow it to count as a record. Nevertheless, she's also won three IAAF Half Marathon Championship titles. She's not bad if you double the distance, either. Name her.

40. These two women have won three Bolder Boulder 10-K races in a row. Both are Olympic Marathon medal winners. Name them.

41. This famous 15K in Tampa Bay has some tenuous connection to a mythical pirate by the name of Jose Gaspar.

42. This American, also a Boston Marathon winner, set a world record for 15-K at the above-mentioned Tampa race, and also a 10-mile record (46:13) at the Cherry Blossom 10-Miler.

A. John A. Kelley; B. Bill Rodgers; C. Craig Virgin; D. Greg Meyer

43. The Comrades Marathon course—approximately 56 miles long—runs from Pietermaritzburg to Durban in "down" years and the opposite way in "up" years. Name the host country for this famous ultramarathon event that began in 1921.

A. The Netherlands; B. Great Britain; C. South Africa; D. Germany

44. Arguably the greatest Comrades runner in the history of the race, this man won the race eight times in the 1980s and set records for both the "up" and "down" courses. Name him.

45. The Western States 100 is definitely her home turf, with seven wins and a course record of 17 hours and change over the rugged mountain trails. She set numerous other ultrarunning records. Who is she?

46. Marathoners run past Tower Bridge and Big Ben in this world-famous event. Name the race.

47. It is now possible to run a race on top of "the Great Wall" in this country.

A. Peru; B. Great Britain; C. China; D. Nepal

48. A highlight of this big city marathon is a dash through the historic Brandenburg Gate.

A. Paris, France; B. Berlin, Germany; C Vienna, Austria; D. Geneva, Switzerland

49. The River Liffey and Phoenix Park figure in the course of this marathon—and good luck to ye, lad!

A. Edinburgh, Scotland; B. Wellington, New Zealand; C. Toronto, Canada; D. Dublin, Ireland

50. The race director of the Chicago Marathon ran a sub-9 minute 2-mile in high school and competed for Villanova in college. Name him.

51. This Roger Bannister teammate and Olympic gold medalist was the man behind launching the London Marathon. Name him.

52. Norwegian Inge Simonsen and this accomplished American deliberately tied for first in the inaugural London Marathon in 1981. Name him.

53. Called the "Tunnel to Towers Run" this New York City 5K honors Stephen Siller, a firefighter who ran through this tunnel wearing 75 pounds of gear on September 11, 2001, and gave his life attempting to save others. Name the tunnel this race goes through.

A. Lincoln Tunnel; B. Brooklyn-Battery Tunnel; C. Columbus Tunnel; D. Downtown Tunnel

RACES BY STATE

54. The Hatfield & McCoy Marathon recalls the historic feud between two infamous mountain clans. The race runs back and forth between what two states?

A. Alabama and Tennessee; B. Georgia and South Carolina; C. North Carolina and Tennessee; D. Kentucky and West Virginia

55. Like former jazz cornet player Bix Beiderbecke, this state's 7-miler (which starts at the Mississippi River in Davenport) hits all the high notes.

A. Iowa; B. Louisiana; C. Missouri; D. Tennessee

56. The Beach to Beacon 10-K includes beautiful scenery—and the Cape Elizabeth course is predictably challenging, since marathon star Joan Benoit Samuelson launched this race.

A. Massachusetts; B. Maine; C. New Jersey; D. Rhode Island

57. The red rocks and camera-worthy scenery help the Garden of the Gods 10-Miler live up to its heavenly name, but relatively high altitude might leave lowlanders huffing and puffing.

A. Utah; B. Wyoming; C. Colorado; D. Idaho

58. You can lace on your blue suede shoes for the "Running with the King 5K" in this state. Shake your hips when you run past Elvis's childhood home in Tupelo.

A. Alabama; B. Mississippi; C. North Carolina; D. Tennessee

59. You can expect to find the Buckeye Classic and the Akron Marathon in this state.

A. Pennsylvania; B. Ohio; C. Iowa; D. Illinois

60. Grin and "Bear" it in this state's 50-mile ultra called Le Grizz—which starts near the Big Sky "metropolis" of Hungry Horse.

A. Alaska; B. Wyoming; C. Montana; D. Idaho

61. The Hood-to-Coast Relay begins on a big mountain, and finishes at the town of Seaside in this state.

A. Alaska; B. Washington; C. California; D. Oregon

62. The Deadwood Marathon and Half-Marathon, the same town where Wild Bill Hickock met his demise holding a poker hand of aces and eights, is held in this state.

A. Montana; B. South Dakota; C. Colorado; D. Kansas

63. The Hemingway Days 5-K is held in this state—one of many places author Ernest Hemingway liked to fish.

A. Alaska; B. Michigan; C. Utah; D. Florida

64. You can chill out at the "Freeze Yer Gizzard Blizzard" races in International Falls—sometimes the nation's "cold spot" on the Weather Channel—in this state.

A. Alaska; B. Maine; C. Montana; D. Minnesota

65. Finish in the top three in your age group in this state's Home Run 10-K, which starts and finishes at the Fargo Krispy Kreme, and you win a box of doughnuts.

A. New York; B. Nebraska; C. California; D. North Dakota

66. The quaint village of Seward is the site of this Fourth of July

event—a scramble up Mount Marathon that dates back to 1915.

A. Alaska; B. Wyoming; C. New Mexico; D. Idaho

67. General Robert E. Lee's first invasion of the North in 1862 led to a horrific one-day battle at Antietam in this state. But you can run a peaceful 10-K there and take in the battlefield monuments as you stride past.

A. Pennsylvania; B. Virginia; C. Kentucky; D. Maryland

68. The race director is fond of describing the Mount Washington Road Race as having "just one hill"—but that "hill" is the highest in this state, and the Northeast.

A. Vermont; B. New Hampshire; C. New York; D. Maine

69. At the George Sheehan Classic 8-K in this state, don't be surprised if you hear someone blasting Bruce Springsteen's "Born to Run" along the course.

A. New York; B. New Jersey; C. Connecticut; D. Pennsylvania

70. Canyon views, low humidity, and some late mile downhills make this state's St. George Marathon an inspired race.

A. Arizona; B. Utah; C. Colorado; D. Nevada

71. Former Olympian Don Kardong was the "brains" (with a little help from Irish author James Joyce) behind the Lilac Bloomsday Run in this state—so blame Don for "Doomsday Hill."

A. Washington; B. Oregon; C. California; D. North Dakota

72. The Cheesehead Half and the Cheese Days Chase might be races you find are to your taste in America's Dairyland (aka "The Badger State").

A. Indiana; B. Illinois; C. Wisconsin; D. Michigan

73. Hills with names like Cardiac, Suicide, and Insult—plus a section of stairway with 671 steps—makes this state's "Dipsea" (a race that dates back to 1905) a challenge.

A. Massachusetts; B. Washington; C. California; D. Oregon

74. This state's beautiful Big Sur Marathon features breathtaking seascape scenery—in addition to a performing string orchestra at the top of a climb.

A. Maine; B. New York; C. California; D. Washington

75. Races such as the Lost Dutchman Marathon, the Whiskey Row Marathon and the White Mountain Half Marathon, that begins in Apache Junction all reflect this Southwest state's history.

A. Arizona; B. Texas; C. California; D. Nevada

76. The Flying Pig Marathon gets off the ground in "the Queen City" in this state.

A. Louisiana; B. Virginia; C. South Carolina; D. Ohio

77. The Country Music Marathon and Half-Marathon are in the city of the Grand Ole Opry in this state.

A. Georgia; B. Oklahoma; C. Kentucky; D. Tennessee

78. Berwick's "Run for the Diamonds" 9-miler—closing in on its 100th running as of this writing—gets the starting gun on Thanksgiving Day in what state?

A. Texas; B. New York; C. Connecticut; D. Pennsylvania

79. The Lake Tahoe Rim 50-K/50-M Trail Run takes in some of the best scenery in the Silver State.

A. Nevada; B. Montana; C. Colorado; D. California

80. The Maggie Valley Midnight Run and the Mount Mitchell Challenge are two scenic challenges in this state.

A. North Carolina; B. Tennessee; C. Indiana; D. Texas

81. The Crim Festival of Races in Flint and the Volkslaufe (People's Run) in Frankenmuth are two well-established races in this Great Lakes state.

A. Wisconsin; B. Michigan; C. Minnesota; D. Ohio

82. The Litchfield Hills 7-Miler—a race that will celebrate its third decade in 2006—starts on the village green of a quaint New England town in this state. But a steep hill in the last mile keeps the runners looking at their shoelaces.

A. Maine; B. Massachusetts; C. Connecticut; D. New Hampshire

83. If you don't know the Great Aloha Run is in this state, then perhaps you have pineapple for brains.

A. Hawaii; B. Florida; C. California; D. Georgia

84. The "Run With the Horses" Marathon takes place in this Cowboy State—one of the least populated in the U.S.A.—but you have a good chance of spotting wild mustangs when you run the race.

A. Montana; B. New Mexico; C. Colorado; D. Wyoming

85. The Alamo Line in the Sand 5-K takes place in this state, commemorating the gallant defenders of the Republic in 1836.

A. Arizona; B. Texas; C. California; D. New Mexico

86. The Green Mountain Marathon in South Hero in this scenic state begins and ends near a house where Clarence DeMar, the seven-time Boston Marathon winner, once lived.

A. New Hampshire; B. Massachusetts; C. Vermont; D. New York

87. This state's potato commission sponsors a several races in May. Alternative rockers the B-52s would be proud!

A. Arizona; B. Maine; C. California; D. Idaho

88. The Caesar Rodney Half-Marathon, named for this state's sign-

er of the Declaration of Independence, is held in this tiny state.

A. Rhode Island; B. New Hampshire; C. Vermont; D. Delaware

89. The Great Cow Harbor 10-K features a beautiful course—and almost everyone must travel east to reach it.

A. Maine; B. New Jersey; C. California; D. New York

90. With six major hills—including an 8.5 percent grade called Trinity—the Hospital Hill Run in this "Show Me" State makes you put up or shut up.

A. Alabama; B. Missouri; C. Colorado; D. Kansas

91. The Lincoln Track Club puts on the nearly three-decade-old Lincoln Marathon—but the lion's share of the running glory in this state still seems focused on the Cornhuskers.

A. Illinois; B. Indiana; C. Nebraska; D. Iowa

92. The Azalea Trail Run and the Cotton Row Run, plus a 5-miler at the Helen Keller Festival, are all races in this Deep South state.

A. Alabama; B. Georgia; C. Mississippi; D. Louisiana

93. A marathon to commemorate the infamous Bataan Death March of World War II takes place on the White Sands Missile Base over high desert terrain in this state.

A. Arizona; B. New Mexico; C. Nevada; D. Utah

94. This state's Hoosier 200-Mile Relay Race begins in Evansville, with the Ohio River as a backdrop, and finishes in Bloomington.

A. Illinois; B. Wisconsin; C. Ohio; D. Indiana

95. If you're a real cowboy, sooner or later you might want to try the Lake McMurtry Trail Run 50-K based in Stillwater in this state.

A. Arizona; B. Texas; C. Colorado; D. Oklahoma

96. Keep an eye out for the Hogeye Marathon, staged in Fayetteville in this state.

A. Arkansas; B. Iowa; C. Tennessee; D. Kentucky

97. The Cherry Blossom 10-Miler takes place primarily in:

A. Atlanta, Georgia; B. Boston, Massachusetts; C. San Francisco,

California; D. District of Columbia

98. The Steamboat 4-Mile Classic in this state has attracted some of the world's fastest runners—answering the question: "Will it play in Peoria?"

A. Arkansas; B. Missouri; C. Mississippi; D. Illinois

99. One of this state's best-known races—a half-marathon—runs through Colonial Williamsburg.

A. Virginia; B. Massachusetts; C. Connecticut; D. Delaware

100. The Newport Mansion 5-K in this state takes you past some big "shacks," including some that appeared in the movie *The Great Gatsby*.

A. Rhode Island; B. New York; C. California; D. Maine

101. The Chickamauga Chase and the Hogpen Hill Climb are races you can run in this state.

A. Arkansas; B. Alabama; C. Georgia; D. Delaware

102. If there weren't so many runners in this state's extremely pop-

ular race, you could dance the Charleston as you finish the Cooper River Bridge Run.

A. Florida; B. South Carolina; C. Georgia; D. West Virginia

103. You can honor the U.S. president and military leader of D-Day when you run the Eisenhower Marathon in this state (Dwight D. Eisenhower's birthplace)—plus run on a course that was part of the historic Chisholm Trail.

A. Texas; B. Pennsylvania; C. Oklahoma; D. Kansas

104. The Paul deBruyn 15-K and 30-K races in this state's Ormond Beach are a memorial to the 1932 Boston Marathon winner from Germany who retired there.

A. Maine; B. Massachusetts; C. South Carolina; D. Florida

105. The oldest race in the South, the Jackson Day race dates back to 1907. It starts at the Spanish Fort and finishes at Old Hickory's statue in Jackson Square in this southern city—commemorating Andrew Jackson's 1815 famous victory over the British, achieved with the help of the infamous pirate Jean Laffite.

A. Savannah, Georgia; B. Jacksonville, Florida; C. Charleston, South Carolina; D. New Orleans, Louisiana

106. On Columbus Day, you can find some of the world's fastest women racing along the Charles River in this state's largest city. The race is the Tufts Health Plan 10-K.

A. Ohio; B. New York; C. Massachusetts; D. Rhode Island

RACES
ANSWERS

1. A
2. C
3. C
4. A
5. A cloth sash worn by each relay runner, then passed on at the exchange zone.
6. *tasuki*
7. The Mini-Marathon
8. D
9. False. It ain't easy, but several women have dipped under 31:00.
10. Grete Waitz of Norway and Tegla Laroupe of Kenya
11. The Boilermaker
12. True
13. Jeff Galloway and Gayle Barron
14. C
15. Ed Winrow
16. Frank Shorter and Bill Rodgers
17. A
18. C
19. B
20. Runs the race without paying an entry fee, often without a

number or with a fake number.

21. D

22. Don Kardong

23. A

24. The Cross-City Race

25. B

26. D

27. C

28. True

29. True

30. C

31. True. But Aussie aces Steve Monoghetti (40:03) and Rob de Castella (40:08) have come tantalizingly close.

32. C

33. Kenny Moore

34. Lisa Martin Ondieki

35. C

36. D

37. B

38. A

39. Paula Radcliffe of Great Britain

40. Rosa Mota of Portugal and Deena Drossin Kastor of the U.S.A.

41. Gasparilla

42. D

43. C

44. Bruce Fordyce

45. Ann Trason

46. The London Marathon

47. C

48. B
49. D
50. Carey Pinkowski
51. Chris Brasher
52. Dick Beardsley
53. B
54. D
55. A
56. B
57. C
58. B
59. B
60. C
61. D
62. B
63. D
64. D
65. D
66. A
67. D
68. B
69. B
70. B
71. A
72. C
73. C
74. C
75. A
76. D
77. D

78. D
79. A
80. A
81. B
82. C
83. A
84. D
85. B
86. C
87. D
88. D
89. D
90. B
91. C
92. A
93. B
94. D
95. D
96. A
97. D
98. D
99. A
100. A
101. C
102. B
103. D
104. D
105. D
106. C

RUNNING IN FILM, LITERATURE, AND ART

You know that running has gone the full circuit when you can find references to it in the Bible *and* in rap music.

In the King James Bible, 1 Corinthians 9:24, the passage reads: "Know ye not that they which run in a race run all, but one receiveth the prize? So run, so that ye may obtain."

And there are at least three or four references to a former track star by rap artists, but that's one of the questions in this section, so . . . no help for you here!

Running, of course, is a near-perfect metaphor for human struggle and human endeavor. As in life, we endure . . . we get through our challenging journeys, and hopefully arrive in a better place. Romans 5:3-4 reads: "We rejoice in our sufferings, because we know that suffering produces perseverance; perseverance, character; and character, hope. And hope does not disappoint us."

More than a few top runners have compared their racing to artistic expression. "For me, running is a lifestyle and an art," says Lorraine Moller, an Olympic marathon medal winner. "I'm far more interested in the magic of it than the mechanics."

Said Gunder Hägg, the fabulous Swedish star of the 1940s: "The runner is another artist, another composer, another poet where the famous paintings, the sublime music or the verses are replaced by world records. Athletics and running become a part of the story and tradition of the whole country in the future."

Even Steve Prefontaine checked in on the runner-as-artist theory. "A race is a work of art that people can look at and be affected by in as many ways as they're capable of understanding," said Pre.

Running, in one form or another, also adapts well to action on the big screen. It's almost as if there's a story within a story—a race has a beginning, middle, and ending. A race can provide action and emotion.

The Russian poet Yevgeny Yevtushenko understood these attributes of physical expression, noting: "True sport is always a duel: a duel with nature, with one's own fear, with one's own fatigue, a duel in which body and mind are strengthened."

And when the body and mind are both strengthened, the creative spirit is sure to soar, bound to flourish—as much passion and art, as it is mere method.

1. In Greek mythology, this fleet maiden was said to have beaten all her male suitors/challengers in a footrace (in one version the "losers" are put to death), until Hippomenes—assisted by Aphrodite, the goddess of love—distracted her by rolling three golden apples off the racecourse. (Hint: A New York City running club for women used her name for their racing team.)

A. Atalanta; B. Artemis; C. Cassandra; D. Helen of Troy

2. The Trojan hero Hector futilely attempts to run away from "swift Achilles"—and certain death—in what epic work that describes their life-and-death footrace around the walls of Troy?

A. William Shakespeare's *Troilus and Cressida;* B. Lewis Wallace's *Ben Hur;* C. Homer's *The Iliad;* D. Homer's *The Odyssey*

3. This Englishman penned a poem about "Pheidippides" (in the late 1870s) and inadvertently helped perpetuate the "myth of the messenger." According to this poet, the runner delivered news of the Greek victory at Marathon to the citizens of Athens—then allegedly dropped dead after shouting: "Rejoice, we conquer!"

A. Robert Browning; B. Lord Byron; C. Samuel Taylor Coleridge; D. Charles Dickens

4. What Athenian playwright described the ancient Olympic Games as "Fair, market, acrobats, fun and thieves" in AD 394?

A. Aristotle; B. Archimedes; C. Plato; D. Menander

5. Better known for detective stories, this writer described the famous collapse of an Olympic marathoner in the 1908 London Games this way: "It is horrible, yet fascinating, this struggle between a set purpose and an utterly exhausted frame."

A. Agatha Christie; B. Ian Fleming; C. Sir Arthur Conan Doyle; D. Franklin W. Dixon

6. This famed mythologist and author (*The Hero with a Thousand Faces* and *The Power of Myth*) counted running track at Columbia University in the 1920s among his fondest memories.

A. Spiro Agnew; B. Robert Graves; C. Joseph Campbell; D. Donald Rumsfeld

7. Mel Gibson and Mark Lee play Australian sprinters who are recruited to be message "runners" in the trenches of World War I in what Peter Weir-directed film?

A. *All Quiet on the Western Front;* B: *Band of Brothers;* C. *Gallipoli;* D. *The Watch on the Rhine*

8. This English poet/runner penned the celebratory poem "The Song of the Ungirt Runners," but soon after was killed in action during World War I.

A. Robert Graves; B. Siegfried Sassoon; C. Charles Hamilton Sorley; D. Dylan Thomas

9. The award-winning *Chariots of Fire* film takes its title from a line

in a poem written by what British poet?

A. William Shakespeare; B. William Blake; C. Alfred Lord Tennyson; D. John Milton

10. The stories of the two runners in *Chariots of Fire* are based upon what two Olympic sprinters?

A. Harold Abrahams and Eric Liddell; B. Reginald Walker and Harry Edward; C. Charley Paddock and Jackson Scholz; D. Jesse Owens and Mack Robinson

11. True or False. W. C. Fields starred in *Million Dollar Legs*—a comedy set at the Olympic Games. He played the president of Klopstockia, who liked to throw the shotput.

12. The fictional English miler of Brian Glanville's novel *The Olympian* is named:

A. Andy Capp; B. Trevor Willingham; C. Colin Warnock; D. Ike Low.

13. What British poet penned "To an Athlete Dying Young" (an ode to a deceased runner of local renown) as part of his *A Shropshire Lad*?

A. A. E. Housman; B. Lord Byron; C. Thomas Hardy; D. Dylan Thomas

14. Most famous for his novel centering on American Irish gangster Studs Lonigan's life in Chicago, this man also wrote a short story (dealing with racial hatred and ignorance) titled "The Fastest Runner on Sixty First Street."

A. John O'Hara; B. James T. Farrell; C. Ernest Hemingway; D. William Butler Yeats

15. An Olympic gold medal winner in the 200 meters in the 1924 Paris Games, this man also wrote a short story about track called "The Winning Bug."

A. Harold Abrahams; B. Eric Liddell; C. Charley Paddock; D. Jackson Scholz

16. A "found object" sculpture called *The Sprinter* appears to be blasting from the starting blocks at the American Sport Art Museum and Archives in Mobile, Alabama. Local artist Bob Larsen constructed this work from discarded hoses, hubcaps, and other scrapped items. *The Sprinter* is a tribute to what great sprinter (a double gold-medal winner) of the 1972 Olympic Games?

A. Armin Hary of West Germany; B. Valery Borzov of the Soviet Union; C. Carl Lewis of the U.S.A.; D. Don Quarrie of Jamaica

17. Originally thought to be a line to create a poem upon, this British writer's *The Loneliness of the Long Distance Runner* blossomed into a short novel.

A. Alan Sillitoe; B. Anthony Burgess; C. Percy Cerutty; D. Rudyard Kipling

18. The antihero/runner in *The Loneliness of the Long Distance Runner*—Colin Smith—is:

A. AWOL from the British army; B. Serving time in reform school for a botched burglary; C. Married to three different women in three different towns; D. Hiding on a remote island off the coast of Ireland after allegedly murdering his father

19. The British actor who played Smith in the film version of *The Loneliness of the Long Distance Runner* very nearly shares the same name with what Olympic champion?

A. James Lightbody; B. Christopher Brasher; C. Tom Courtney; D. Daley Thompson

20. The movie *Running Brave* details the trials and triumphs of what famous Olympic champion?

Tom Longboat; B. Billy Mills; C. Jim Thorpe; D. Louis Tewanima

21. The lead role in *Running Brave* was played by

A. Mel Gibson; B. Robby Benson; C. Richie Cunningham; D. Robert De Niro

22. Name two films (one that helped catapult his career to a new level and the other a 1976 thriller based on the novel by William Goldman) starring famed actor Dustin Hoffman that have a running connection.

23. Name the 1994 blockbuster film in which Tom Hanks's character literally runs "cross-country."

24. Name the three-word phrase from this film that is sometimes yelled from car windows to taunt runners.

25. What 1970 film (adapted from Hugh Atkinson's novel of the same name) brought together the *Love Story* author (Erich Segal) and actor (Ryan O'Neal) in a plot about four marathoners vying for Olympic fame?

A. *The Games;* B. *The Pheidippides Paradox;* C. *The Laurel Wreath;* D. *The Marathon Men*

26. Name the obsessive British coach—who preaches to his runner that a sub-2-hour marathon is possible—in the above novel/film?

A: Alfred Lord Thomas; B. Harry Hayes; C. Percy Cerutty; D. Sam Dee

27. More famous for his alleged love of guns and substance abuse, this recently deceased "gonzo" journalist once "covered" the Honolulu Marathon—his essay accompanied by charmingly-grotesque drawings from the pen of Englishman Ralph Steadman appearing in the short-lived magazine *Running*.

A. Keith Moon; B. Hunter Thompson Jr.; C. Truman Capote; D. Tom Wolfe

28. This cartoon poked fun at long-distance runners in 1978 when the high-mileage, brain-addled Dr. Miles Potash—author of *The Complete Book of Pain*—was introduced.

A. "Garfield" (Jim Davis); B. "Peanuts" (Charles Schultz); C. "Cathy" (Cathy Guisewite); D. "Doonesbury" (Garry Trudeau)

29. The Disney movie *The Incredibles* introduced this fleet little character, a rival for any Olympic sprinter.

A. Atomic Adam; B. Blinding Speed; C. Cruise Missile; D. Dash

30. A Newbery Medal-winning book, Cynthia Voigt's *The Runner,* which involves a high school runner destined for the Vietnam War, is primarily aimed at younger readers but finds its mark with readers of all ages. The protagonist's speedy nickname is:

A. Rocket; B. Bullet; C. Missile; D. Dart

31. Better known for his novel *One Flew Over the Cuckoo's Nest,* this late writer—an Oregon graduate—was chosen as the narrator for *Fire on the Track: The Steve Prefontaine Story.*

A. Allen Ginsberg; B. Jack Nicholson; C. Neal Cassidy; D. Ken Kesey

32. This documentary of the 1972 Olympic Games brought together a "dream team" of photographers to capture the Olympics from many different angles.

A. *Visions of Eight;* B. *Berlin Stories;* C. *Olympia;* D. *The Games of Joy and Sorrow*

33. This former Florida Track Club runner wrote the cult classic *Once a Runner.*

A. John Parker; B. Jack Bacheler; C. Jimmy Carnes; D. Jeff Galloway

34. The protagonist/miler in *Once A Runner* is named:

A. Archie Hamilton; B. Ike Low; C. Quenton Cassidy; D. Jimmy Falcon

35. Robert Towne has directed two films that involve running/track athletes. Name them.

36. Name the Olympic distance runner (he just missed a medal at Munich in 1972) who had a part in *Personal Best* as a water polo player interested in the female lead?

A. Jack Bacheler; B. Kenny Moore; C. Ron Clarke; D. Don Kardong

37. Two other American track stars—one a top marathon runner, the other a great hurdler—had cameo appearances in *Personal Best*. Name them.

38. A prolific actor with dozens of films to his credit (including roles in the award-winning *Ordinary People* and the collegiate classic *Animal House*), this man played Oregon Coach Bill Bowerman in

Without Limits.

A. Tim Matheson; B. Kevin Bacon; C. Dustin Hoffman; D. Donald Sutherland

39. Ed O'Neill played Coach Bill Dellinger in the 1997 Steve James directed film *Prefontaine,* but he might be more noted for playing what role in a long-running television series?

A. Al Bundy from *Married With Children;* B. *Bonanza*'s Little Joe; C. Norm from *Cheers*; D. Cowboy Rowdy Yates from *Rawhide*

40. GOLD-MEDAL QUESTION. Ross Lockridge Jr. wrote a best-selling novel in 1948 (later to become a movie of the same name starring Mongomery Clift and Elizabeth Taylor) in which a key scene features a Fourth of July footrace between protagonist Johnny Shawnessy and his fleet-footed, hard-drinking rival "Flash" Perkins. Name that historical novel, set in the Civil War era.

A. *Gravity's Rainbow;* B. *Gone with the Wind;* C. *Raintree County;* D. *Glory*

41. Ross Lockridge Jr. knew something about running because he ran cross-country at Indiana University, where he was a teammate (and rival in the courtship of the woman who eventually became Lockridge's wife) with this collegiate star and two-time Olympic 800-meter finalist.

A. Jim Spivey; B. Terry Brahm; C. Charles Hornbostel; D. Malvin Whitfield

42. A statue of what Canadian sprint star (a former 100-yard and 100-meter world-record holder, and an Olympic bronze-medal winner) breasts an imaginary finish line in Vancouver's Stanley Park?

A. Tom Longboat; B. Ben Johnson; C. Harry Jerome; D. Jerome Drayton

43. A plaque on the monument dedicated to this sprinter reads: THE WILL TO DO, THE SOUL TO DARE. These inspirational words were written by what famous Scottish poet/novelist? (Hint: He wrote *Ivanhoe*—not *Trainspotting*.)

A. Sir Walter Scott; B. Robert Burns; C. Irvine Welsh; D. Dylan Thomas

44. Also in Vancouver is a statue of this Canadian sprint star— winner of the 1928 Olympic 100-meter gold—but he's depicted in starting-line crouch. Name him.

45. There's a bronze statue of this Irish American marathon runner—an Olympic champ—in Nenagh, County Tipperary, Ireland, the birthplace of his parents. Name the marathoner.

46. Not only is there a statue in her honor outside Bislett Stadium in Oslo, but she also has been featured on a Norwegian stamp. Name this great runner.

47. Which of these famous poets did *not* write a poem about running?

A. W. H. Auden; B. Walt Whitman; C. Richard Wilbur; D. A. E. Housman; E. They all wrote poems about running

48. The Federal Republic of Germany eventually showed a "de-Nazified" version of this director's highly acclaimed 1938 documentary of the 1936 Berlin Olympic Games—a film that perhaps surprisingly included shots of African American sprint jump star Jesse Owens.

A. Albert Speer; B. Leni Riefenstahl; C. Werner von Braun; D. Wolfgang Petersen

49. Better known for his roles in *Fatal Attraction, Basic Instinct,* and *Wall Street,* he played Michael Andropolis in this 1979 flick about a marathon man with Olympic ambitions. Although the actor took

some 10-mile-plus training runs to look the part, this film—*Running*—basically "hit the wall" and failed to attract many viewers. Name the actor.

A. Michael J. Fox; B. Kevin Bacon; C. John Cusack; D. Michael Douglas

50. This 1974 bestseller by Patricia Nell Warren—arguably one of the first novels involving same-gender love to break into the mainstream market—revolved around the relationship between a young runner and his coach.

A. *The Front Runner;* B. *In Dubious Battle;* C. *Racing in the Key of Life;* D. *Stonewalls*

51. Actor Henry Fonda outlegs his warrior pursuers to warn the settlers in this 1939 John Ford blockbuster (based on a historical novel of the same name by Walter D. Edmonds) in a memorable life-or-death cross-country race. Name the movie.

A. *Fort Apache;* B. *Little Big Man;* C. *Dances with Wolves;* D. *Drums Along the Mohawk*

52. True or False. A number of rap artists have used lines about "Flo Jo" in their songs.

53. Regarded by many as "The Dean of American Songwriters," this man wrote a song about the Italian marathoner Dorando Pietri shortly after the 1908 Olympic Games. It was one of his first successes. Name this famous composer, better known for "White Christmas."

A. Aaron Copeland; B. Irving Berlin; C. Leonard Bernstein; D. Harry Von Tilzer

54. After this sprinter won the 1976 Olympic Games 100-meter dash, Calypso songs—among other honors—were written for him. (Hint: He was this island country's very first Olympic champion.)

A. Lennox Miller of Jamaica; B. Silvio Leonard of Cuba; C. Hasley Crawford of Trinidad; D. Donald Quarrie of Jamaica

55. Already well on the way to victory in 1984, Joan Benoit Samuelson picked up some late-race inspiration about half a mile from the stadium. What was it?

A. A song being played over the loudspeaker system; B. a huge painted mural depicting her crossing the Boston Marathon finish line; C. a spectator with a MAINE T-shirt; D. her husband-to-be was cheering for her from a street corner

56. Prior to the 2004 Olympic Games in Athens, New Balance Athletic Shoe, Inc., commissioned statues to present to the village of Marathon—start of the Olympic Marathon. The work—a 10-foot high bronze statue by Mico Kaufman—depicts two famous Greek marathoners Spiridon Louis (1896 winner) and Stylianos Kyriakides. What did the latter runner accomplish, and for what specific cause?

57. The Finnish sculptor Eino created an inspiring piece of art called *The Last Meter*—depicting the furious and close finish of the 1976 Olympic 5000-meter run won by Lasse Viren. The original work was on display in this city's Piedmont Park.

A. Atlanta; B. Boston; C. Lucerne, Switzerland; D. New York City

58. In the 1983 classic *Risky Business,* Rutherford (who is interviewing Joel (played by a young Tom Cruise) for possible admission to Princeton and says: "You've done a lot of solid work here, Joel, but it's just not Ivy League, now, is it?") reads the high school senior's list of accomplishments. Most of them are lame, but what is the one that readers of this book might applaud?

59. The New Millennium HBO hit *Six Feet Under* showed numerous scenes of what character (he's a reluctant undertaker in his working life) out running?

60. Riding the wave of the running boom, this how-to book by a former overweight advertising writer sold nearly a million copies in the late 1970s. Name the author and the book.

61. This doctor-turned-running philosopher—a miler at Manhattan College in his younger days—also put a book on the bestseller list in the late 1970s. Name the author and his work.

62. In 1996 the U.S. Postal Service issued a stamp (designed by San Francisco artist Michael Bartalos) expressing the joy of running. This stamp was issued to commemorate what major event?

A. Bay to Breakers; B. The 100th running of the Boston Marathon; C. The New York City Marathon; D. The Atlanta Olympic Games

RUNNING IN FILM, LITERATURE, AND ART
ANSWERS

1. A
2. C
3. B
4. D
5. C
6. C
7. C
8. C
9. B

Bring me my bow of burning gold!
Bring me my arrows of desire!
Bring me my spear! O clouds unfold!
Bring me my chariots of fire!

10. A
11. True
12. D
13. A
14. B
15. D
16. B
17. A

18. B

19. C

20. B

21. B

22. *The Graduate* (in which Benjamin Braddock is noted to have been "captain of the cross-country team") and *Marathon Man,* which shows clips of Ethiopian great Abebe Bikila.

23. *Forrest Gump*

24. "Run, Forrest, run!"

25. A

26. B

27. B

28. D

29. D

30. B

31. D

32. A

33. A

34. C

35. *Without Limits* (on Prefontaine) in 1998 and *Personal Best* (the fictional piece that stars Mariel Hemingway as a budding heptathloner) in 1982.

36. B

37. Frank Shorter and Edwin Moses

38. D

39. A

40. C

41. C

42. C

43. A

44. Percy Williams
45. Johnny Hayes
46. Grete Waitz
47. E
48. B
49. D
50. A
51. D
52. True. These include Sir Mix-A-Lot's "Baby Got Back" ("I'll keep my women like Flo-Jo . . . ") and Ludacris ("Stay on track, hit the ground runnin' like Flo-Jo . . ." There are others, too.)
53. B
54. C
55. B
56. He won the 1946 Boston Marathon, specifically wishing to draw attention to a life-threatening food crisis in postwar Greece.
57. A
58. "One year of varsity track."
59. Nate Fisher, played by Peter Krause
60. Jim Fixx and *The Complete Book of Running*
61. Dr. George Sheehan, *Running and Being*
62. B

FINISH LINES
(Odds & Ends)

In his book *A Clean Pair of Heels,* Murray Halberg of New Zealand, after winning an Olympic gold medal, wrote: "I had always imagined an Olympic champion was something more than a mere mortal, in fact, a god. Now I knew he was just a human being."

Halberg meant, more or less, that runners who work hard—in a reasonably intelligent and consistent way—are quite capable of great achievements. Dream races and, yes, even Olympic medals aren't necessarily awarded to those blessed with supernatural talent.

By the same token, being an accomplished runner doesn't necessarily shield one from the full slate of life's problems. As mere mortals, runners aren't "bulletproof"—though on those rare days, sailing along at top speed, we might swear that we are—that nothing can touch us! However, as I collected trivia questions for this book, I was stunned by how many great runners had died in warfare or conflict, how many had suffered fatal or crippling, career-ending car crashes, how many despite their earlier renown ended their lives smothered and crushed by poverty. You could, in fact, form an all-star team of great runners whom the Fates later turned their back upon.

In some ways, running is an expression against our own mortality. To paraphrase Sam Dee, the eccentric coach (a Cerutty-type figure) in Brian Glanville's fine novel *The Olympian,* we can never totally defeat death; the stopwatch itself tells us that with each sweep of the second hand. But we confirm our fighting spirit and dignity every time we lace on our running shoes and rage against our complacency, our lethargy, our melancholy.

"Running is a lot like life," said David Bedford, the British runner who trained like a maniac and once set a world record for 10,000 meters. "Only ten percent of it is exciting. Ninety percent of it is slog and drudge."

But we live for that 10 percent. And we try to face "the rest of it" with courage and dogged determination—like a stitched-up fighter who rallies from his dark corner in the late rounds, and refuses to toss in the blood-flecked towel when all the evidence strongly suggests otherwise.

"A lot of people run a race to see who's the fastest. I run to see who has the most guts," said the late Steve Prefontaine, gone from us and the sport he loved at age twenty-four.

When you take on the challenges of running—and even the challenges of life—those are good, solid words to etch upon your battle shield.

1. "That's not Frank! That's an imposter!" screamed this *Love Story* author/television color commentator at the Munich Olympics. Entering the stadium shortly after, Frank Shorter was perplexed by the shrill whistling (the European equivalent to "booing") that actually wasn't meant for him—but for a German prankster. But who was the writer from Yale who was so infuriated?

2. Name the 17-year-old California kid who won the Olympic decathlon in 1948.

A. Andrew Lloyd Webber; B. Bob Mathias; C. Sean Combs; D. Dan O'Brien

3. This funny guy—and a great athlete—once wryly described the decathlon as "nine Mickey Mouse events and a 1500."

A. Jim Thorpe of the U.S.A.; B. Bruce Jenner of the U.S.A.; C. Milt Campbell of the U.S.A.; D. Daley Thompson of Great Britain

4. Name the German athlete who assisted Jesse Owens in the 1936 Olympic Games. He helped Owens get his steps right for the long-jump approach, although it might have cost the German a gold medal.

5. Olympic flags flew at half-mast after this tragedy at the Munich Olympic Games in 1972.

6. Just a day after it was announced this city would host the 2012 Olympic Games, it was struck by a terrorist attack.

A. Madrid, Spain; B. Bali, Indonesia; C. New York City; D. London, England

7. In 2003 Abeselom Yihdego, an Ethiopian philanthropist, paid to construct a statue of a recently deceased Olympian from his country. The statue was placed next to another statue of another great runner in the St. Joseph Church yard in Addis Ababa, the capital city. Name the two runners honored.

8. In 1987 this great Olympic runner was honored as a "Sportsman of the Year" by *Sports Illustrated* because of his humanitarian efforts with orphaned youth in his country. Name him.

9. **BRONZE-MEDAL QUESTION.** In 1980 this Canadian dipped his leg in the Atlantic Ocean and began the 5,300-plus cross-continent "Marathon of Hope." Several statues in Canada now honor him, including a 9-foot bronze at Thunder Bay, overlooking Lake Superior. Name him.

10. This Canadian hero's style of running was dubbed what?

11. The last Olympic gold medals made entirely out of that precious metal were awarded in:

A. 1896; B. 1912; C. 1936; D. 1968

12. What city is known to fans as "TrackTown U.S.A."?

A. Philadelphia, Pennsylvania; B. Boston, Massachusetts; C. San Jose, California; D. Eugene, Oregon

13. This famous comedian, a former top-notch track athlete at Temple University, has always been a big supporter of the Penn Relays. Name him.

14. Which U.S. president once had a rough day in a 10-K road race and was forced to drop out of the event? The pictures of his distress were wildly circulated.

A. Gerald Ford; B. Rutherford B. Hayes; C. Jimmy Carter; D. William Howard Taft

15. This U.S. president was in the White House and supported the Moscow Olympic Games boycott.

A. Richard Nixon; B. Lyndon Baines Johnson; C. Jimmy Carter; D. Gerald Ford

16. Which of these countries didn't attend the Moscow Olympic Games—in essence, supporting American foreign policy?

A. Australia; B. Great Britain; C. Cuba; D. Kenya

17. Filbert Bayi of Tanzania—the world-record holder in the 1500 meters at the time—didn't get to race at the Montreal Olympic Games because:

A. He injured his Achilles tendon in training; B. Most of the black African countries boycotted the 1976 Olympic Games; C. He was suffering from a recurring bout of malaria; D. He false-started

18. Despite some great successes (and a famous marathon finish against Alberto Salazar), bad luck—in the way of serious injuries from a car accident and a dangerous mishap with farm machinery—hastened the end to this man's world-class racing career. Name him.

19. Which of these things did Mary Decker Slaney *not* do in her career?

A. Fling a baton in anger at a Russian runner; B. Blame Zola Budd for her fall in the Los Angeles Olympics 3000 meters; C. Win an Olympic bronze medal in the 1500 at Montreal in 1976; D. Win the 1500- and 3000-meter world championship races in 1983— henceforth known as "The Double Decker"; E. Set an American record for 10,000 meters

20. "You can't eat trophies," quipped this two-time Boston Marathon champion. He finished his life living in poverty, and died in an altercation outside a bar. Name him.

21. SILVER-MEDAL QUESTION. This 1928 Olympic marathon champion who ran for France was fatally shot in 1959 by members of the Algerian Liberation Movement outside a Paris café because he refused to support their cause. Name him.

22. This Olympic marathon champ named his daughter "Olympia."

A. Alain Mimoun of France; B. Paavo Nurmi of Finland; C. Emil Zatopek of Czechoslovakia; D. Juan Carlos Zabala of Argentina

23. In a bit of a surprise, this American runner—a winner at New York and Boston in the previous decade—won the Comrades Marathon (a 54-mile "ultra") in 1994 in 5 hours, 38 minutes. Who was this marathon man?

A. Alberto Salazar; B. Bill Rodgers; C. Craig Virgin; D. Frank Shorter

24. This famous Olympic distance runner wasn't the only great athlete in his house. His wife, Dana, won an Olympic gold in the javelin in 1952.

A. John Landy of Australia; B. Gordon Pirie of Great Britain; C. Emil Zatopek of Czechoslovakia; D. Vladimir Kuts of the Soviet Union

25. Alan Webb has a tattoo on his right shoulder. What is it?

A. Nike's "swoosh" logo; B. A block letter M for Michigan; C. A Chinese character; D. A "Roadrunner" bird

26. If talk show queen Oprah Winfrey, rap star Sean "Diddy" Combs, and comedian Will Ferrell ran a marathon, who—judging from their PRs (that's "personal records" not "public relations"!)—who would win?

27. More than 100 "Race for the Cure" events—fund-raiser runs to raise awareness and fight breast cancer—take place around the country. The races also are in honor and memory of this woman.

28. Runners for Team in Training usually meet the patient for whom they are running to raise funds. What disease does Team in Training take on?

29. GOLD-MEDAL QUESTION. In the Olympic Marathon in Rome in 1960, whether by coincidence or design, Abebe Bikila of Ethiopia made his final move of the race about a mile from the finish line in the Colosseum—just when he pulled alongside the obelisk of Axum. Explain the significance of obelisk of Axum.

30. Ethiopian great Abebe Bikila wore shoes when he won the 1964 Olympic Marathon. But what brand of running shoes were they?

A. Adidas; B. Reebok; C. Tiger; D. Puma

31. The 1960s in track and field was marked by a fierce rivalry between two German brothers who led their respective sporting shoe companies. Name the two companies.

32. This famous American distance runner had an indoor track at Yale named in his honor.

33. This great American sprinter had to fend off accusations of accepting illegal expenses when he appeared without "authorization" in the 1923 University of Paris Games. The NCAA helped him beat the rap and appear in the Olympics the next year.

A. Calvin Smith; B. Bob Hayes; C. Charley Paddock; D. Jackson Scholz

34. In the 1920s and 1930s, Mary Pickford and Douglas Fairbanks attended Olympic competitions and encouraged their favorite athletes—such as sprinter Charley Paddock. Who were they?

A. Famous Hollywood actors; B. U.S. Congressional representatives; C. Famous clergy; D. Famous jazz musicians

35. In 1933 this great long sprinter—a star in the 1932 Olympics and still very much in his prime—broke his legs in a horrific car crash. He was unable to run outdoor track his senior year at Penn. Who was he?

36. True or False. If Texas was its own country in Olympic competition, the number of track-and-field medals won by athletes either born in the state or who have spent their competitive years in the state outstrips all but three countries in the world, excluding the U.S.A.

37. In 1896 Australian Edwin Flack won two gold medals on the track and attempted (with less success) to run the marathon. What other Olympic sport did he participate in?

A. Archery; B. Basketball; C. Tennis; D. Darts; E. Equestrian

38. There's a statue of this man—complete with painter's cap—near an entrance to Central Park and not far from the New York Road Runners Club headquarters. Name this promoter of the sport.

39. What world-class runner helped pace the man (right answer to the previous question!) to his first five-borough New York City Marathon finish in 1992?

40. When his shoe company did not renew contract—just two days before he was to race the New York City Marathon—this marathon runner decided to wear a plain white singlet. He crushed the field by more than 3 minutes, clocking 2:08:20.

A. Alberto Salazar of the U.S.A.; B. Steve Jones of Great Britain; C. Carlos Lopes of Portugal; D. Rob de Castella of Australia

41. "I ran for myself, never for Finland," said this man. Nevertheless, he was regarded as a national hero. Name him.

42. In 1994 this Olympic distance king put his gold medals up for sale, claiming: "The medals have no sentimental value for me. What does it matter if they are with me or with someone else?"

A. Paavo Nurmi of Finland; B. Lasse Viren of Finland; C. Waldemar Cierpinski of East Germany; D. Emil Zatopek of Czechoslovakia

43. A very uncharacteristic sixth-place finish in the 1990 Commonwealth Games convinced this Olympic middle-distance great it was time to retire. "I feel like a boxer who looks great in the gym, but

as soon as he enters the ring he gets knocked out. But then this is no longer life or death for me." Name him.

A. John Walker of New Zealand; B. Sebastian Coe of Great Britain; C. Steve Cram of Great Britain; D. Rod Dixon of New Zealand

44. With great courage, this Olympic hero said: "In the days of my victory and joy I had Faith enough to thank the Lord. Now as well, I should not but accept my accident in Grace." Name this two-time Olympic champion.

45. This runner was such a "dark horse" that when he crossed the finish line first in the 1964 Olympic 10,000-meter race, a Japanese official blurted out: "Who are you? Who are you?" So who was he?

46. When this Olympic hero passed away, he had six Olympians serve as his pallbearers. There's a bronze statue of him outside the Olympic stadium in his country's capital—and in 1952 he ran in with the Olympic torch, to thunderous applause. He's depicted on his country's 10-mark note.

47. "Remember me to my Olympic Brothers!" exclaimed the 1968 Olympic marathon champion and bronze medalist in 1972, when this American writer and former Olympian attempted to gain his release from an Ethiopian prison. (Hint: The African runner nipped the American for the last medal in Munich.) Name them both.

FINISH LINES
ANSWERS

1. Erich Segal
2. B
3. D
4. Ludwig "Lutz" Long
5. The murder of Israeli athletes at the hands of Palestinian terrorists
6. D
7. Abebe Bikila and Mamo Wolde
8. Kipchoge "Kip" Keino
9. Terry Fox. With one leg amputated from cancer, he attempted to average 26 miles a day to raise money and awareness to fight the disease. He died before he could complete the journey. Canadians honored him in many ways, including $24 million in pledges.
10. "The Fox Trot."
11. B
12. D
13. Bill Cosby
14. C
15. C
16. D
17. B

18. Dick Beardsley
19. C
20. Ellison "Tarzan" Brown
21. Boughera El Ouafi
22. A
23. A
24. C
25. C. Reportedly it stands for courage, strength, and bravery.
26. Go with the funny guy, Will Ferrell.
27. Susan G. Komen
28. Leukemia
29. The Italian army had looted this sacred religious artifact from Ethiopia when they invaded that country in the 1930s under Fascist ruler Mussolini's orders, and brought it to Rome. It was only recently returned to Ethiopia, transported in sections because it weighs 160 tons.
30. D
31. Adidas and Puma
32. Frank Shorter
33.
34. A
35. Bill Carr, the Olympic champion at 400 meters in Los Angeles.
36. True. Texans have won more Olympic track-and-field medals than most countries. Only the Soviet Union, Great Britain, and Finland have won more, if you don't count the U.S.A.
37. C
38. Fred Lebow
39. Grete Waitz of Norway
40. B

41. Paavo Nurmi
42. B
43. B
44. Ethiopia's Abebe Bikila, following a 1969 car crash that left him paralyzed.
45. Billy Mills
46. Paavo Nurmi
47. Mamo Wolde and Kenny Moore